Everything's OK

Prologue

The world we inhabit, from the quiet dance of electrons to the grand arcs of galaxies, brims with complexity. At first glance, this complexity can seem overwhelming, random, or beyond our grasp. Yet, woven into its intricate patterns lies a profound reassurance: complexity is not barren chaos; it tends toward meaningful, stable configurations. The human mind's capacity for reason, the endurance of ethical virtues over centuries, the resilience of cultural traditions, and the strength of enduring friendships and alliances—all hint at a universal principle in action. Where infinite possibilities unfold, certain filters, criteria, and frameworks guide them into coherent forms.

This principle, though subtle, is everywhere. It governs how tiny particles find stable states that underpin matter's solidity and chemistry's richness. It shapes how societies discover moral codes that reinforce trust, how individuals refine their moral compasses to achieve lasting peace of mind, how communities converge on stable agreements, and how global negotiations yield enduring alliances. Across these varied domains, from the microscopic to the cosmic, from personal introspection to diplomatic accords, stable complexity emerges whenever honesty, openness, empathy, and rational consideration reduce friction and uncertainty.

In this understanding, moral and intellectual virtues are no longer quaint ideals reserved for saints or philosophers; they become strategic necessities. Integrity, fairness, compassion—these values are not accidental ornaments of civilization but structural features that ensure complexity produces life-sustaining patterns rather than turmoil. Their repeated success in guiding complexity toward stable outcomes affirms their role as rational solutions, tested and validated by history's long scrutiny.

This perspective does not promise a perfect world or painless progress. Challenges remain, mistakes occur, and setbacks demand recalibration. Yet each trial teaches lessons, refining the filters and principles that manage complexity. Over iterative cycles, as more actors align with honesty, reasoning, and empathy, complexity's infinite potential becomes a resource rather than a burden. Problems that once paralyzed societies become puzzles solvable through trust-based dialogue. Personal anxieties that once gnawed at the soul ease, replaced by quiet confidence that complexity can be navigated toward coherent results.

In the pages that follow, we examine this logic of complexity alignment as it appears in human life, nature, and thought. We explore how recognition of stable complexity patterns can change our approach to decision-making, moral growth, cultural development, scientific inquiry, and even our understanding of existential purpose. Far from an esoteric theory, this logic acts as a lens that clarifies every domain it touches, guiding the mind through complexity's intricate terrains and illuminating the stable, meaningful outcomes attainable with ethical coherence and rational foresight.

This is not a call to naive optimism, but a reasoned affirmation that everything—a negotiation, a community project, a moral dilemma, a creative venture—can find stable resolution if guided by clarity, sincerity, and adaptive intelligence. From this vantage point, complexity ceases to intimidate. It invites engagement, promising that patient, ethical alignment will reveal patterns both reliable and humane. Here, complexity becomes the canvas upon which human potential and moral aspiration paint their finest achievements.

(End of Prologue)

CHAPTER 1: THE ZERO-POINT OF KNOWING (PART A)

A single, undeniable fact: I think, therefore I am. This foundational statement, distilled from centuries of philosophical probing, is more than a clever phrase. It represents an anchor against the tumult of doubt. Strip away all assumptions about your surroundings, memories, cultural teachings, or scientific claims, and still you cannot deny the reality of your own awareness. No matter how radically you question existence, the act of questioning confirms a questioning entity—yourself.

This certainty, though minimal, contains a profound implication. Consciousness, the capacity for reflective thought, does not arise in a vacuum of pure chaos. For you to perceive, reason, and hold stable identities and memories, there must be some underlying order that allows such processes to emerge and persist. If reality were an unfathomable chaos of arbitrary states, it would not sustain coherent observers, let alone thinking beings capable of introspection. That you exist as a self-aware entity suggests that complexity—no matter how vast—holds within it the capacity for stable patterns, rules, and structures. In other words, the mere fact of your conscious awareness implies that the universe's complexity is not raw confusion but complexity channeled into coherent forms.

Consider how delicate this balance is. Your mind weaves

sensory data, past experiences, and new information into a continuous narrative. Without stable principles enabling this narrative, thoughts would fragment instantly into incoherent noise. Something must guarantee that signals are interpretable, that some patterns repeat reliably, that causal relations hold consistently enough for logic and memory to function. Even if you know nothing else for certain, your very thought process testifies that you do not float in senseless chaos.

From this baseline understanding emerges a critical insight: complexity need not be tamed by brute force. It already contains tendencies or selection criteria that favor stable configurations. Conscious awareness, reasoning, and perception are not miraculous intrusions; they reflect structural conditions that permit complexity to manifest as meaningful states. This acknowledgement transforms your perspective. Instead of viewing yourself as stranded in an arbitrary cosmos, you see your conscious faculties as products of a universe inclined toward coherence.

This reasoning marks a pivot away from philosophical skepticism. While skepticism strips away unreliable beliefs, leaving "I think, therefore I am" as a last certainty, it seldom provides a constructive path forward. Here, however, that same certainty opens a door: if your existence as a reasoning entity is secure, and reasoning requires stable complexity, then complexity's nature must support such stability. Complexity, therefore, is not an enemy to human comprehension but a substrate through which patterns and intelligible structures continuously emerge.

This realization undercuts existential anxieties that might arise from confronting the unknown. If you trust that complexity inherently supports stable cognition, then the unknown is not necessarily a threat. Instead, it is a domain where further stable patterns can be discovered, so long as one navigates complexity with principles that harness its potential. Your consciousness stands as proof that complexity has already been harnessed successfully at least once: in the formation of your intellect and self-awareness.

Deep comfort can stem from this recognition. Though the universe may still present challenges—phenomena not yet understood, social tensions not yet resolved, personal dilemmas not yet settled—you know complexity holds the capacity for stable resolutions. Your mind's coherence is a microcosm of a broader logical tendency: infinite possibilities being filtered into stable, meaningful outcomes. Far from a random swirl of events, reality contains the seeds of order and intelligibility.

At this stage, you might naturally wonder: If stable complexity allows for consciousness and thought, could it also shape moral values, scientific order, or social ethics? The logic that supports your introspective capacity might also guide the formation of trustworthy institutions, reliable knowledge, and sustainable communities. This possibility arises not from wishful thinking, but from following the initial logic of complexity's structural support. If consciousness can emerge and persist, who's to say that complexity alignment does not also underpin other coherent patterns that humanity seeks?

For now, focus on the baseline: you exist, you think, and therefore complexity must contain tendencies conducive to stable cognition. This sets a tone of cautious optimism: complexity is not an impenetrable riddle but a field where stable states are both possible and, in your own existence, already realized. Your awareness thus acts as both a fact and a clue, indicating that behind the veil of uncertainty, a framework or logic ensures that complexity does not spiral endlessly into nonsense.

Embracing this fact prepares you for deeper inquiries. Recognizing that stable complexity underlies reason and awareness encourages you to ask how such stable complexity might influence moral reasoning, collaborative efforts, predictive strategies, and long-term plans. All those questions can be approached with greater confidence once you accept that complexity, by necessity, gives rise to coherent forms rather than unending disorder.

CHAPTER 1: THE ZERO-POINT OF KNOWING (PART B)

The insight that your awareness implies structured complexity is more than a philosophical comfort. It suggests a foundational principle: whenever complexity manifests stable, coherent states —like your self-reflective consciousness—these states result from some manner of underlying logic or filter. Without such logic, complexity would devolve into arbitrary chaos, incapable of sustaining observers or yielding consistent experiences.

This line of reasoning infuses the pursuit of knowledge with a subtle but powerful optimism. If the basic fact of your thinking self is tied to order within complexity, then investigating the world is not a futile endeavor. Each attempt to understand phenomena—physical laws, social dynamics, biological processes —seeks patterns that complexity alignment allows to form. You are not blindly guessing; you are working with a universe predisposed, at least in part, to produce recognizable and analyzable structures. This predisposition undergirds the confidence that truth-seeking efforts—science, philosophy, moral reasoning—can yield genuine insights.

Consider how this perspective might affect your approach to unfamiliar problems. Suppose you encounter a moral dilemma you cannot resolve immediately. Instead of concluding that morality is a hopeless tangle, you recognize that if stable complexity fosters meaningful states in other domains, it should also guide you toward ethically coherent resolutions. If at first clarity eludes you, it may be due to incomplete information, biased assumptions, or insufficient empathy. Refining these filters —seeking more data, questioning assumptions, opening yourself to compassion—moves you closer to stable moral outcomes that align with complexity's logic.

Similarly, when wrestling with intellectual puzzles—scientific anomalies, conceptual paradoxes, technological uncertainties— you do not assume a hostile universe determined to thwart understanding. On the contrary, the fact that complexity permitted a rational mind to arise encourages the belief that complexity also allows rational solutions to emerge. Each puzzle challenges you to refine your cognitive tools. By persisting, gathering better data, or rethinking interpretations, you coax stable knowledge structures out of infinite possibilities. Over time, repeated successes confirm that complexity can indeed be systematically navigated and understood.

This viewpoint also has subtle existential implications. It counters the notion that human existence is a fragile accident adrift in meaningless complexity. While it does not claim a grand purpose preordained by external forces, it does assert that the conditions enabling conscious reflection are woven into reality's fabric. In a universe where complexity leans toward stable, intelligible outcomes, your existence as a conscious knower is not a perverse fluke but a natural expression of that tendency. This recognition can diminish feelings of cosmic alienation or absurdity, replacing them with a sense of belonging to a cosmos that, at least in some crucial respects, supports rather than undermines understanding and meaning.

Embracing this perspective also enriches interpersonal relations. Awareness that complexity alignment underlies stable cognition can encourage you to seek clarity, honesty, and constructive engagement in conversations. If communication is honest and empathetic, misunderstandings and conflicts—forms of complexity friction—can be minimized. Over time, this approach yields more stable, trusting relationships, mirroring the logic that brought forth coherent consciousness from infinite possibilities. Just as stable complexity in your mind enables rational thought, stable complexity in social interactions emerges when all parties strive for transparency and goodwill.

By starting from a single certainty—"I think, therefore I am"—and unfolding its implications, you have established a philosophical and emotional baseline. Complexity is not to be feared as an unknowable maze; it can be navigated through principles that produce coherence and durability. Your own conscious life demonstrates that complexity can yield stable, meaningful states. With that assurance, you can move into any domain—moral, intellectual, social, practical—armed with the knowledge that the universe's complexity is not indifferent or impenetrable. Instead, it provides conditions ripe for pattern formation, stable outcomes, and ongoing discovery.

The zero-point of knowing—that kernel of certainty embedded in your self-awareness—serves as a permanent reference. Whenever doubts resurface, remember that if your very capacity to doubt proves your existence as a reflective agent, it also proves complexity's capability to sustain rational observers. This realization inspires confidence: you have a starting line from which to explore complexity's depths, trusting that no matter how intricate the challenge, there is a pathway toward stable, comprehensible states. In this way, the fundamental truth of your own awareness becomes a guiding star, orienting you toward complexity-managed insights and reassuring you that what you seek—understanding, moral coherence, creative solutions—stands on the same logical ground that made thinking minds possible in the first place.

CHAPTER 2: COMPLEXITY, ETHICS, AND COHERENCE (PART A)

Having acknowledged that conscious awareness implies a universe capable of producing stable complexity, we turn now to a fundamental question: how do ethical principles emerge from this intricate interplay of patterns and possibilities? If stable outcomes are favored by the structure of complexity itself, it stands to reason that the behaviors and norms that reduce friction, enhance trust, and foster cooperation should naturally arise, survive, and spread. Ethics, far from a fragile social construct, may instead reflect the structural advantages conferred by coherence in a complexity-rich environment.

At first glance, ethics and complexity might seem unrelated. Ethics concerns how individuals treat one another, how societies form moral codes, and how values endure over time. Complexity, on the other hand, describes the interwoven relationships of innumerable components—particles in a system, agents in a market, citizens in a community. Yet the gap between the moral and the structural is bridged by the realization that stable complexity states do not arise from randomness alone. They require filters that eliminate patterns prone to chaos and conflict. Ethical principles perform such filtering roles in human affairs, much as physical constraints and feedback loops do in natural phenomena.

To see this in action, consider the role of trust. In a low-trust environment, individuals must devote tremendous energy to verifying information, guarding against deception, and enforcing contracts. Every interaction adds layers of friction—extra steps, safeguards, and deterrents—just to achieve basic cooperation. This friction consumes resources and generates instability: infinite possibilities cannot settle into stable patterns easily because too many potential states involve mistrust, cheating, or hidden agendas that escalate complexity into disorder.

In a high-trust environment, by contrast, complexity is handled more efficiently. Agreements form more readily, information flows more openly, and creative collaborations emerge without the constant drag of suspicion. Trust acts like a complexity lubricant. By reducing friction, it allows potential states to be filtered through a simpler and more direct set of criteria. The result: stable relationships, enduring institutions, and predictable markets. Ethical values such as honesty and reliability, therefore, aren't merely moral niceties. They serve as critical complexity filters, trimming away fractious patterns and enhancing the likelihood that societies find stable, supportive equilibrium states.

This perspective reframes morality as more than a cultural preference or spiritual teaching. Instead, it is a structural necessity to manage complexity efficiently at the human scale. While countless potential social configurations exist— from hierarchical oppressive regimes to egalitarian networks of cooperation—the configurations that last tend to be those in which ethical coherence reduces friction and unpredictability. Over generations, ethical norms become internalized, passing from one era to the next as cultural wisdom. People find it natural to say "honesty is the best policy" not just because it sounds good, but because societies where honesty prevails repeatedly prove more resilient and prosperous.

Empathy offers another example. Without empathy, social complexity tilts toward misunderstanding, alienation, and conflict. Disputes fester, groups splinter, and complexity spirals into cycles of retribution or hostile competition. Empathy, by guiding individuals to recognize and respect the inner worlds of others, reduces these complexities. It enables more stable patterns of reconciliation, cooperation, and mutual aid. Empathy thus functions as a moral compass that directs social complexity into configurations that are easier to maintain and enrich over time. In this sense, empathy's value is not only emotional or spiritual—it is structurally rational, a complexity-alignment tool that fosters constructive and enduring social landscapes.

Fairness, too, emerges as a complexity-friendly principle. When resources, opportunities, and responsibilities are distributed justly, friction diminishes. People trust that efforts and contributions will be acknowledged, that no hidden manipulations skew outcomes unfairly. Such fairness increases predictability, lowers stress, and encourages long-term planning. Societies with fair norms find it simpler to integrate new members, absorb shocks, and adapt to changing conditions. Conversely, where unfairness reigns, uncertainty and tension proliferate. Over time, these unstable states either collapse or force corrections that restore a more balanced, fair arrangement. Thus, fairness isn't an abstract moral goal; it's a strategic imperative embedded in the structural logic of complexity management.

These insights demonstrate that ethical coherence emerges not as a random moral preference but as a natural selection criterion acting within social complexity. Just as physical systems settle into stable orbits or chemical equilibria, social systems, given time, discover ethical frameworks that minimize energy wasted on conflict and mistrust. Ethical values stand as complexity's enduring beacons—signals that a community has learned, through historical trial and error, that certain moral standards yield reliable stability and long-term viability.

CHAPTER 2: COMPLEXITY, ETHICS, AND COHERENCE (PART B)

Ethical principles do not spontaneously appear fully formed. They evolve through collective learning, cultural exchange, and historical experimentation. Early societies might stumble upon codes of reciprocity or hospitality out of necessity. Over time, these rudimentary moral codes refine themselves. Interactions that reduce complexity friction spread, while those that multiply confusion and conflict fade. Traditions that encourage respecting guests, sharing surplus harvests, or resolving disputes peacefully persist because they produce stable and predictable benefits for all parties involved. In this way, moral norms are distilled from the infinite set of possible social behaviors, with complexity alignment acting as the silent hand selecting which patterns endure.

Consider how civilizations have often converged on similar moral insights despite differing religious doctrines, linguistic backgrounds, or economic conditions. Concepts like truth-telling, fairness, and kindness recur across countless cultures. This cross-cultural moral convergence suggests that these values are not arbitrary or confined to a single historical context. Instead, they represent recurring solutions to the universal problem of navigating social complexity. Each culture, facing its unique challenges, discovers that certain ethical behaviors yield stable outcomes. Over many generations, these values become embedded in laws, myths, educational systems, and everyday customs, making them integral parts of social identity.

This realization enriches the concept of moral progress. Moral progress is not merely an accumulation of lofty ideals but a series of structural improvements in complexity management. As societies learn to implement more transparent governance, respect minority rights, or ensure equitable resource distribution, they eliminate patterns of wasteful friction and needless suffering. The moral "advancement" recorded in historical annals reflects an increase in predictability, trust, and stability at the social level. Ethical enhancements thus stand as strategic upgrades to complexity filters, making it easier for communities to thrive amid ever-changing conditions.

Such ethical advancements also encourage the formation of trust networks that can operate at scales larger than kinship ties or immediate neighborhoods. When trust extends across regions or nations, possibilities multiply exponentially. Trade routes open without fear of rampant fraud, alliances form without the shadow of immediate betrayal, and cultural exchanges proceed without mutual suspicion. This global ethical coherence reduces complexity friction at international scales. Diplomatic relations become more productive, scientific collaborations more fruitful, and cultural fusions more harmonious. Over time, these trust-based patterns become durable elements of human civilization's complexity handling, guiding efforts to address global challenges with rational confidence and moral clarity.

At the individual level, understanding that ethics correlates with complexity coherence provides a fresh lens for personal moral struggles. When tempted by dishonest shortcuts or self-serving manipulations, one can reframe these temptations as short-term gambits that impose hidden complexity costs. These costs might not appear immediately, but they accumulate as relational tension, reduced credibility, or compromised well-being. Conversely, acts of honesty, compassion, and fairness solidify stable patterns in one's personal life. Over repeated instances, these patterns yield more reliable friendships, more meaningful work experiences, and a greater sense of inner peace. Recognizing that moral virtue is not just morally righteous but structurally advantageous supports sustained ethical effort, even when it demands patience or courage.

Ethics, then, moves beyond superficial codes of conduct imposed by authority. Instead, it emerges as a dynamic, complexity-sensitive logic discovered and refined by societies seeking lasting stability. This complexity-rooted interpretation of morality can also ameliorate the tension between moral relativism and moral absolutism. While surface expressions of morality vary across cultures, the underlying function—reducing complexity friction—remains constant. Thus, beneath moral diversity lies a shared structural imperative. Different societies may adopt distinct rituals or customs to implement fairness or compassion, but the purpose they serve, the reduction of complexity friction, is universal. This perspective provides a rational basis for inter-cultural moral dialogue, encouraging openness to different paths that achieve similar stability benefits.

This understanding also influences how we conceive institutions like courts, parliaments, councils, or educational bodies. If stable complexity outcomes arise from ethical coherence, designing institutions that embody ethical transparency and inclusiveness is not just idealism—it's strategic engineering. Just as architects consider structural physics when erecting stable buildings, institutional designers must consider ethical physics, the principles ensuring their frameworks channel complexity efficiently. Failure to integrate honesty or fairness into institutional design results in corruption, inefficiency, and eventual instability, just as ignoring gravitational forces leads to architectural collapse.

A nuanced appreciation of ethics as complexity alignment also clarifies why certain moral failures, no matter how cleverly disguised, cannot sustain long-term success. Exploitation might appear to yield immediate gains, but it stores complexity friction like a pressure building behind a dam. Eventually, that pressure forces systemic adjustments, either through rebellion, collapse, or reform. Historical cycles of corrupt regimes toppled by popular uprisings or monopolistic practices undone by market upheavals are testaments to this structural inevitability. Ethical coherence thus becomes a measure not just of moral virtue but of strategic prudence.

In sum, seeing ethics as arising from complexity's structural demands transforms moral reasoning into a grounded, purposeful enterprise. Moral principles are not arbitrary commandments or fragile ideals; they are tested solutions that have repeatedly shown their capacity to convert complexity from chaos into sustainable order. By understanding morality in this way, individuals gain a deeper appreciation for honesty, empathy, and justice, and societies become more confident in choosing ethical reforms. This stable foundation encourages both moral innovation and steadfast adherence to proven ethical norms, forging a path toward durable well-being and resilient cultural progress.

CHAPTER 3: THE S-Φ-P TRIAD (PART A)

If the capacity for stable complexity informs consciousness and ethical coherence, what underlying mechanism ensures that endless possibilities yield clear, coherent outcomes? To navigate complexity effectively at any scale, one must understand how infinite states become manageable events. Introducing a conceptual triad can help: a structure that shows how infinite potentials are sorted, refined, and selected into stable, observable realities. This triad, composed of three conceptual nodes—S (Singularity), Φ (Pharmonic Field), and P (Plane of Incidencion)—offers a lens through which to interpret the transformation from possibility to actuality.

Consider first the idea of S (Singularity). The Singularity represents the boundless realm of what could be—every conceivable configuration of matter, thought, action, or state of affairs. It is an abstract notion of total potentiality, encompassing far more than just physical arrangements. Cultural possibilities, moral frameworks, social policies, innovative ideas, and personal choices all lie folded into S. Infinite complexity resides here, not yet constrained or channeled. S is raw possibility without form, order, or selection.

Without some principle of selection, the vastness of S would be paralyzing. Complexity would remain a theoretical promise rather than a lived reality. That's where Φ (Pharmonic Field) enters. The Pharmonic Field can be imagined as a dynamic filtering environment, a set of criteria or processes that test and sort through the infinite potentials in S. Φ is not a single entity, but a conceptual operator that examines states, discards those that fail to form coherent patterns, and amplifies those that resonate with underlying principles of stability. It functions somewhat like a musician tuning strings to find harmonious notes within an infinite range of frequencies. Rather than brute force, it relies on feedback, harmony, and resonance to identify patterns capable of enduring. In physical contexts, natural laws, feedback loops, and energy minimization principles act like Φ. In social or moral domains, trust, honesty, empathy, and rational deliberation serve as filters, pruning chaotic possibilities and guiding the selection of more stable social outcomes.

Finally, P (Plane of Incidencion) represents the actualized result—the manifested outcome of complexity selection. When potentials pass through Φ and emerge as stable events, they appear on P. This plane encompasses all that is actual, from observable physical phenomena (like a particle detected at a specific location) to the tangible decisions societies implement (like a law enacted after much debate), and even personal choices (like a resolved moral dilemma resulting in a concrete action). P is where theory meets practice, where infinite possibility condenses into a single, coherent moment of reality.

The significance of this triad lies in its universality and adaptability. It does not confine itself to a single domain, like physics or morality. Instead, it provides a general template for understanding how complexity—always abundant and often overwhelming—is refined into workable solutions. Whether analyzing the crystallization of a mineral structure, the resolution of a diplomatic impasse, the settling of ethical norms in a community, or the creative process in an artist's mind, the triad shows that infinite states (S) are subject to filtering processes (Φ) that yield stable, chosen outcomes (P).

This conceptual structure also underlines why trust in certain filters or criteria is warranted. If time and again stable results emerge from applying transparent guidelines, fair negotiations, and honest data-sharing, then these elements clearly serve as effective components of Φ. They help distinguish viable states from nonsensical or destructive patterns. Over iterative cycles, successful filtering strategies become entrenched as cultural wisdom, scientific principles, or personal habits, making future complexity handling smoother and more predictable.

CHAPTER 3: THE S-Φ-P TRIAD (PART B)

Consider how the S-Φ-P triad manifests across different scenarios. In physics, quantum fields present infinite potential states (S) for particles. Certain conditions—like energy minima, symmetry principles, and measurement interactions—act as Φ, selecting stable states that appear on P as observed particles with definite properties. In social domains, any community may propose countless solutions (S) to a shared problem, but filters such as reasoned debate, ethical standards, and evidence-based arguments (Φ) guide the group to a stable agreement (P) that endures.

This triad does not claim that all complexity is immediately tamed or that every chosen outcome is perfect. Instead, it reveals a pattern: whenever complexity yields stable results, some filtering operation has occurred. The complexity filters need not be static; they adapt as conditions change. In evolving societies, ethical frameworks sharpen over time as lessons from past decisions refine what counts as a stable, good outcome. Similarly, in science, theories evolve as new data refine our filtering criteria, discarding old assumptions that no longer fit stable patterns.

This capacity for refinement is crucial. If the Singularity (S) represents a boundless sea of possibilities, then Φ must also be flexible and open to revision. A filter that never adapts might miss emerging opportunities for even more stable states or fail to account for newly discovered complexities. Infinite testability and continuous refinement ensure that the Pharmonic Field (Φ) remains attuned to shifting conditions, whether environmental changes, cultural transformations, or intellectual breakthroughs. This dynamic responsiveness allows P, the manifested plane of results, to remain rich in meaningful patterns, rather than ossifying into brittle outcomes unsuited to changing realities.

Ethical coherence and rational deliberation often appear as parts of Φ at human scales. When trust-based negotiation repeatedly leads to stable accords, we learn that honesty and empathy are effective complexity filters. Over generations, societies come to expect moral alignment as a standard feature of complexity handling. The triad helps explain why moral and rational values gain such durability: they have proven their utility as filtering mechanisms that produce stable, beneficial outcomes over and over again.

Similarly, at personal scales, when an individual faces confusion or moral uncertainty, they may rely on reflective thought and empathetic reasoning—internal filters—to sift through emotional surges and conflicting desires. Through trial and experience, they identify which mental habits lead to stable inner peace and productive decisions. In this process, personal virtues form as mental filters refined by experience, guiding the selection of thoughts and actions that yield harmonious life events.

The triad also grants a framework for predicting and improving future states. By studying how certain filters in Φ have historically led to stable outcomes on P, one can infer which new filters might prove fruitful. Whether developing fair policies to handle a looming environmental crisis or designing better scientific instruments to glean stable patterns from quantum experiments, the logic of complexity selection guides the creation or improvement of complexity filters. Over iterative cycles, filters improve, predictions become more accurate, and achieved outcomes more resilient.

Crucially, S-Φ-P suggests a universe that is not static or deterministic in a simplistic sense. Instead, it embraces the idea that infinite potentials interact with adaptive filtering criteria to yield reality's stable tapestry. This interaction is dynamic: as lessons are learned, filters adjust, and new stable states emerge. The result is a universe conducive to progress and moral development, not just mechanical repetition. Complexity can be harnessed ethically and intelligently, ensuring that as conditions evolve, outcomes improve in tandem.

From a philosophical standpoint, the triad offers a language to discuss how possibility transforms into reality without relying on mystical explanations or rigid determinism. It does not deny contingency; it acknowledges that infinite states exist. Nor does it deny structure; it insists that stable patterns arise through selective filtering. This balance between endless potential and guided selection helps make sense of phenomena that once seemed mysterious or arbitrary. Patterns in ecosystems, stable social contracts, enduring moral principles, creative achievements—all can be mapped onto the interplay of S, Φ, and P.

By internalizing the S-Φ-P triad, individuals and communities gain a mental model for interpreting complexity. Instead of feeling overwhelmed by the infinite possibilities life presents, one can look for appropriate filters and trust that stable outcomes will emerge. This perspective can reassure that with the right ethical frameworks, rational deliberation, and openness to feedback, complexity need not be chaotic or threatening. Instead, it is a fertile field from which coherent, meaningful states continually arise, so long as we learn how to cultivate and refine the filters that guide them.

In essence, the triad stands as a conceptual cornerstone, reminding us that infinite possibilities (S) by themselves do not suffice to produce order. It is the filtering process (Φ)—ranging from physical symmetries to ethical norms—that chooses from

S and plants stable outcomes on P. This recognition empowers us: we are not helpless before complexity, but active participants shaping it through our chosen filters. Over time, as we apply and improve these filters, we increasingly align ourselves with stable, enriching patterns, ensuring that complexity remains a source of constructive evolution rather than confusion.

CHAPTER 4: FROM QUARKS TO GALAXIES—PHYSICS THROUGH THE LENS OF COMPLEXITY ALIGNMENT (PART A)

The logic of complexity alignment does not confine itself to human affairs or ethical considerations. Its influence extends into the very fabric of physical reality, guiding how matter arranges itself, how forces interact, and how stable cosmic structures form. Understanding complexity alignment in physics reveals that the underlying principles encouraging coherence and stable outcomes are not human inventions but fundamental tendencies. From the tiniest subatomic particles to vast galactic systems, complexity alignment suggests that stable configurations emerge wherever infinite potential states are filtered by the laws of nature into durable patterns.

Begin at the quantum scale. Quantum fields present a sheer abundance of possible states for particles—energy levels, spin orientations, positions, momenta. Without constraints, these possibilities would remain abstract potentials, never condensing into observed events. Yet particles do appear with well-defined properties. Electrons occupy stable orbitals around nuclei, photons propagate predictably, and atomic spectra show consistent patterns. This order arises because natural laws, acting like complexity filters, eliminate unstable or incoherent quantum states. Energy minima, symmetry principles, and conservation laws serve as the filters, ensuring only viable particle states materialize as measurable events. Each detection of a particle in a particular state can be viewed as complexity alignment at work—an infinite set of potential outcomes narrowed to a stable, meaningful one.

Scaling upward, the same logic appears in molecular formation. Atoms interact through electromagnetic forces, exploring countless arrangements. Not every arrangement yields a stable molecule; most potential configurations drift apart or fail to achieve bonding. Yet a few discrete patterns, such as the familiar structures of water, carbon dioxide, or complex organic molecules, remain consistently favored. These stable molecular geometries, achieved through intricate electron sharing and energy minimization, arise because physical forces and quantum constraints filter out chaotic arrangements. Complexity alignment ensures that molecular complexity does not remain a formless jumble but settles into recognizable, reproducible structures with properties that persist across conditions. The stability of molecular patterns underpins chemistry, biology, and ultimately life itself.

Push further to the scale of stars, planets, and galaxies. Initially, cosmic matter after the Big Bang was a near-uniform distribution of particles, a chaotic sea of potential formations. Gravity, density fluctuations, and thermodynamic processes acted as complexity filters. Regions with slightly higher density drew in more matter, reinforcing gravitational wells. Over eons, stars ignited under the pressure of gravitational collapse. Galaxies formed from rotating clouds of gas and dust, settling into coherent spirals, ellipticals, or irregular shapes. These stable cosmic arrangements are not the result of arbitrary happenstance; they reflect how physical laws continuously filter infinite potential distributions of matter and energy, yielding stable, self-sustaining entities. Complexity alignment here is evident in the enduring patterns of cosmic architecture—galaxies that hold their form for billions of years, star clusters that maintain gravitational equilibrium, and planetary systems that find stable orbits.

Observing these phenomena reveals that complexity alignment is embedded in nature's deepest workings. Without stable attractors —energy minima, equilibrium states, resonance conditions— physical complexity would offer no reliable frameworks. The chaos of infinite possibilities would never condense into the stable, law-abiding world we study and inhabit. Instead, we find that from quantum fields to galaxy clusters, stable outcomes consistently emerge, confirming that complexity can be managed and made coherent through inherent filtering processes. This realization instills confidence that reality's complexity is not an impenetrable riddle but a structured stage where predictable patterns can be discovered, understood, and harnessed.

—

CHAPTER 4: FROM QUARKS TO GALAXIES—PHYSICS THROUGH THE LENS OF COMPLEXITY ALIGNMENT (PART B)

The lessons from quantum and cosmic structures confirm that stable complexity patterns emerge wherever underlying conditions filter potential states into coherent outcomes. In quantum realms, the filtering criteria include symmetry operations, probabilistic rules of wavefunctions, and interactions between fields and observers. At large scales, gravitational frameworks, thermodynamic principles, and conservation laws play similar roles, guiding matter and energy distributions into lasting formations. In both cases, complexity alignment is not optional—it is the very reason reality can exhibit order rather than perpetual randomness.

This perspective can enrich understanding of natural constants and physical laws. Consider that fundamental constants, like the speed of light or the gravitational constant, contribute to defining complexity filters. If these constants differed radically, stable atoms or stars might never form, and complexity would remain unorganized at that scale. The delicate balance of these constants suggests that complexity alignment is woven into the very fabric of physical law. Instead of viewing the universe as a neutral stage where anything could happen, one sees it as a sculpted arena where complexity alignment continuously molds chaos into recognizable, reproducible patterns.

The role of time in physics also gains a nuanced interpretation. Time provides a dimension along which complexity alignment unfolds. Systems evolve through states, and filtering processes sort through infinite possibilities moment by moment, selecting stable trajectories. Over extended periods, these trajectories accumulate into reliable narratives: stable planetary orbits that persist for billions of years, molecular structures that maintain their integrity under various conditions, ecological networks that remain in dynamic equilibrium. The passage of time thus becomes integral to complexity alignment, allowing patterns to reinforce themselves or be replaced by superior, more stable alternatives.

In fields like condensed matter physics, complexity alignment explains why certain phases of matter—solids, liquids, gases, superconductors—are not random outcomes but specific stable solutions chosen from a vast phase space. Cooling a material below a certain temperature, for instance, can induce a quantum ordering that filters the system's states into a superconducting phase. This transition represents complexity alignment at work: the system discards all non-coherent, higher-energy, friction-laden configurations in favor of a low-friction, stable order that defies classical limitations. Predicting such transitions involves understanding how complexity alignment manifests in specific conditions, thereby making complex material properties not just surprising discoveries but logically inferred results of underlying filters.

In cosmology, complexity alignment underpins the growth of

structure. After the Big Bang, matter and radiation filled space uniformly. Over immense spans of time, subtle imbalances and feedback loops guided matter into gravitational wells, forging galaxies and star clusters. Observing these patterns—the distribution of galaxies along filaments and voids—offers direct evidence that complexity does not remain featureless. Instead, it settles into large-scale coherence. Astronomers and cosmologists find stable complexity patterns in rotation curves of galaxies, in the self-similar hierarchies of structures, and in the longevity of these forms. Complexity alignment ensures that not all cosmic matter is destined to diffuse into uniform chaos; rather, it can arrange itself into meaningful cosmic tapestries, each stable configuration reinforcing the logic of structured selection.

Another implication arises when considering how complexity alignment might guide the search for life elsewhere in the universe. The emergence of life, depending on complex molecular and environmental conditions, may also reflect complexity filters that encourage stable biochemical networks over non-viable alternatives. While life involves chemistry and biology, the foundational principle that infinite potentials are honed by effective filters suggests that if the conditions align —energy sources, stable molecular bonding, and protective niches—complexity alignment can foster life's stable metabolic and replicative patterns. Though this remains speculative, it illustrates how thinking in terms of complexity alignment broadens the understanding of how stable patterns might arise even in exotic environments.

On a philosophical note, acknowledging complexity alignment in physics dispels notions that the universe is indifferent to order. Although not implying any conscious intention behind natural laws, it does show that certain organizational principles are intrinsic. Complexity alignment reveals that fundamental interactions and constants do not yield absurd or meaningless outcomes. They refine chaos into coherence, making comprehension possible and stable phenomena abundant. This shift from viewing the universe as arbitrarily complex to inherently structured encourages intellectual optimism. If complexity alignment can manifest stable galaxies and reliable atomic structures, then no domain—be it new areas of physics, undiscovered states of matter, or unexplored cosmic frontiers—is beyond the reach of patient exploration guided by honest inquiry.

In practical terms, understanding complexity alignment in physics supports more effective scientific inquiry. When researchers develop models of particle interactions or cosmic evolution, they implicitly rely on complexity alignment. Their theories assume that certain solutions are stable, that certain symmetries hold, and that observed patterns are not freak accidents but repeated confirmations of stable complexity outcomes. Each discovery—such as new particle resonances or gravitational waves—reinforces that complexity logic is dependable. Adjusting theories to incorporate unexpected results is less a sign of failure than a natural step in refining the filters that decode complexity into predictable forms.

Ultimately, complexity alignment in physics exemplifies how infinite possibilities find stable expression. From the quantum foam to the grand dance of galaxies, stable configurations testify to underlying regularities. This universality encourages bridging insights across fields, as the logic that ensures stable molecular bonds or cosmic architectures may inspire methods of managing complexity in social systems, ethical dilemmas, or personal decision-making. Knowing that complexity can be made coherent, and that nature demonstrates this fact continuously, fuels a sense of unity between scientific observation and the broader quest for stability, meaning, and understanding in a world rich with potential.

CHAPTER 5: ETHICS, SOCIETY, AND THE EMERGENCE OF GOOD (PART A)

Societies, composed of individuals with diverse intentions and backgrounds, present a level of complexity far exceeding that of simpler systems. In human communities, cultural norms, institutional rules, moral codes, and shared values must somehow coalesce into stable, enduring patterns. Without some guiding principle, the sheer abundance of possible social configurations could descend into chaos—endless conflicts, rampant mistrust, and wasted potential. Yet history and observation show that societies often achieve order, predictability, and long-term cooperation. This orderly complexity suggests that ethical coherence—principles like honesty, fairness, empathy—are not just moral ideals but structural necessities for navigating social complexity effectively.

Consider the nature of complexity within a community. Every interaction—be it a commercial transaction, a political debate, a family dispute, or a cultural exchange—adds variables and expands the possibility space of what can happen next. If these interactions occurred without any principles favoring stability, complexity would remain a source of confusion and volatility. Instead, we see that certain norms reduce friction. Trust, for example, allows people to assume that others will act reliably, cutting down on endless verification steps and protective measures. This simplification is profound: trust acts like a stabilizing force, selecting patterns of cooperation and reducing the infinite set of malicious or deceitful options to a smaller, manageable set of actions conducive to harmony.

When trust and ethical honesty permeate a society, complexity does not vanish—it becomes more productive. Markets run smoothly when participants believe in fair dealings, reducing transaction costs and fostering innovation. Educational systems flourish when students trust that their efforts lead to recognition and skill-building, rather than exploitation. Political institutions gain legitimacy when citizens trust that decision-making occurs transparently, with everyone's well-being in mind. Across all these domains, ethical standards serve as complexity filters, sifting out unstable states—deceit, corruption, oppressive rules—that generate unnecessary friction and push societies toward collapse or reform.

This perspective reveals that ethical norms evolve as pragmatic solutions to complexity dilemmas. Over time, communities discover that certain moral values enhance predictability and reduce uncertainty. Early in human history, tribes that practiced some form of reciprocal kindness or established taboos against betrayal likely found it easier to maintain cohesion and adapt to challenges. Groups without such ethical grounding may have splintered under internal strife, failing to harness the potential of their complexity. Thus, moral norms do not arise solely from spiritual revelation or philosophical decree; they emerge as tested strategies for complexity management. Those that consistently yield stable, peaceful, and prosperous outcomes become entrenched in cultural memory, passed down as virtues and upheld by legal frameworks.

This grounded view of ethics also clarifies why certain moral principles appear universal. Concepts like truth-telling, hospitality, fairness, and protection of the vulnerable recur across countless cultures, ages, and belief systems. These universal moral themes can be understood as convergent solutions to a shared structural problem: how to channel the complexity of social life into stable, life-enhancing patterns. Whenever humans face the infinite range of possible behaviors, they find themselves repeatedly drawn to rules that minimize harmful unpredictability. Over centuries, societies refine these rules, confirming that they reduce complexity friction and guide social states toward durable equilibrium.

Understanding ethics as a structural response to complexity enriches the concept of moral progress. Instead of viewing moral evolution as a mysterious moral awakening, see it as iterative improvement in complexity handling. Societies learn from crises: when authoritarian oppression or rampant dishonesty produce chaos, cultural lessons form. These lessons encourage reforms—like establishing fair courts, protecting civil liberties, or ensuring honest media—that restore predictability and trust. In this sense, moral advancement mirrors technical or scientific progress: an ongoing refinement process that filters out unworkable social patterns and strengthens coherence. The moral trajectory of humanity can then be read as a journey of complexity alignment, each major ethical reform confirming that stability and ethical coherence go hand in hand.

CHAPTER 5: ETHICS, SOCIETY, AND THE EMERGENCE OF GOOD (PART B)

If moral principles emerge as complexity filters at the social scale, then what do they look like in practice? Consider trust once more. Trust, sustained by honesty and fairness, is not a vague ideal but a strategic advantage. In its presence, agreements form swiftly, resources flow efficiently, and creative collaborations flourish. The complexity of negotiations and collective decision-making becomes manageable because all parties operate on shared ethical ground. Each instance of fulfilled promises and transparent dealings reinforces trust, creating a self-reinforcing cycle. Over repeated interactions, trust solidifies into a cultural expectation, and that expectation, in turn, reduces complexity friction even further.

Empathy offers another instructive example. Empathy enables individuals to anticipate the emotional states, needs, and vulnerabilities of others. Without it, social complexity tends toward fragmentation: misunderstandings go unaddressed, conflicts escalate, and the delicate networks of human relationships become strained. Empathy, by encouraging perspectives that consider others' experiences, broadens the set of stable outcomes. Instead of unresolved tensions that corrode social bonds, empathy paves the way for restorative solutions and mutual understanding. Such stability is a precious currency in any collective setting, improving the quality of communal life and ensuring that the infinite potentials of human interaction yield supportive and nurturing states.

Fairness is similarly pivotal. Without fair opportunities and just rules, complexity devolves into power struggles and manipulative maneuvering. This friction wastes resources and intellectual capital, as actors must constantly guard against exploitation. Fair systems, by contrast, assure participants that their contributions and efforts stand a reasonable chance of success. Over time, these systems accumulate human talent and goodwill, fueling sustained development. Stable outcomes under fairness are not only ethically pleasing; they are strategically superior, minimizing the chaos that unfairness spawns and ensuring that cooperative solutions remain viable and adaptive.

These examples highlight that ethical coherence, at its core, harmonizes complexity. By reducing fear, suspicion, and competitive sabotage, moral norms make it easier for societies to predict outcomes, plan for the future, and maintain equilibrium under changing conditions. Ethical principles thus become standards against which infinite social possibilities are measured and refined. Policies that increase transparency or improve accountability become widely accepted because they consistently yield stable, prosperous arrangements. In a world where complexity can otherwise overwhelm, these moral anchors are indispensable.

Considering historical patterns, one sees that when societies drift too far from ethical coherence—through corruption, intimidation, secret deals, or manipulative propaganda—they eventually face internal turmoil. Unrest flares, trust evaporates, and resource misallocations multiply. Complexity, deprived of effective filters, overwhelms the social order, leading to crises and demands for reform. Reforms typically reintroduce or strengthen moral standards, restoring honesty and fairness to reduce friction and stabilize the system anew. Over centuries, this cyclical correction process teaches a key lesson: ethical coherence is not optional if stable social complexity is to be sustained. It is a structural imperative.

On a practical level, this understanding guides policymakers, community leaders, and everyday citizens. When shaping new initiatives—whether community projects, business regulations, or educational reforms—integrating ethical considerations is not a luxury but a strategic move. Emphasizing open-data policies, fair dispute resolution mechanisms, and inclusive representation in decision-making directly aligns with complexity logic. These measures preempt many forms of friction, thereby fostering outcomes that are not just ethically commendable but pragmatically stable. Predictably, such ethically guided approaches win out over time, as evidenced by higher social trust, improved well-being, and longer-lasting cultural achievements.

This perspective also alters how individuals approach moral dilemmas. Instead of treating ethics as abstract commandments or burdensome constraints, one sees them as navigational aids in complexity's ocean. Being honest, for instance, is not just morally right; it is complexity-smart, increasing your predictability to others and building reputational capital. Over time, that reputational capital translates into better networking opportunities, supportive relationships, and reduced uncertainty. The personal payoff aligns with the moral virtue because they are both facets of stable complexity filtering in action.

Empathy and fairness similarly enhance personal and collective stability. Responding empathetically to someone's distress is not merely kind; it stabilizes your immediate social environment, reducing the risk of misunderstandings or resentments that could fester and erupt later. Acting fairly, whether in dividing rewards or assigning responsibilities, prevents seeds of jealousy and mistrust from taking root. By aligning personal conduct with complexity principles, you find greater ease and coherence in everyday life, experiencing less tension and reaping the consistent benefits of stable complexity patterns.

In sum, understanding ethics as arising from complexity's structural demands reveals that moral conduct, trust, empathy, and fairness are not incidental virtues. They are the tested, rational criteria that filter the infinite chaos of human interaction into stable, manageable, and uplifting social states. This realization validates long-standing moral traditions and universal moral themes as grounded in rational necessity rather than whim. It imbues moral striving with renewed confidence: if societies that invest in honesty and compassion repeatedly thrive, then moral investment is not just worthwhile, it is indispensable.

Wherever infinite possibilities challenge the coherence of social life, ethical principles stand ready as complexity selectors. They ensure that from this abundance, stable, life-enhancing patterns emerge. This structural view of ethics, grounded in complexity alignment, encourages more deliberate moral cultivation, more trust in honest dialogue, and more faith in cooperative solutions. By acknowledging that ethical coherence is essential for stable complexity management, humanity gains a stable foundation upon which to build enduring prosperity, peace, and cultural resonance.

CHAPTER 6: CONSCIOUSNESS, AGENCY, AND SELF-AWARENESS (PART A)

Consciousness stands as a defining enigma of human existence. To possess self-awareness is not simply to exist, but to know that one exists, to reflect upon thoughts, feelings, and decisions. This capacity grants individuals a unique vantage point: they are not passive elements adrift in complexity; they are active interpreters, decision-makers, and shapers of reality's unfolding patterns. Understanding consciousness and agency against the backdrop of complexity reveals that your inner world—the realm of reflections, aspirations, and moral considerations—is deeply woven into the very logic that governs the universe's stability.

Agency, the ability to choose and influence outcomes, emerges naturally once we realize that infinite potential states can be navigated rather than endured. Just as physical forces or social trust networks filter vast possibilities into stable events, your mind operates as a local complexity filter. You consider countless thoughts, desires, and impulses—some fleeting, others compelling—and select from them to form coherent plans, judgments, and actions. This selection process is not haphazard; it aligns with the same structural imperatives that shape stable galaxies or thriving communities. Where external reality uses physical laws or ethical constraints to guide stable complexity, your consciousness uses rationality, empathy, memory, and learned values to refine internal potentials into constructive decisions.

Self-awareness sharpens this process further. To be aware of your thoughts is to observe complexity in action—countless mental states arise, from emotional surges to intellectual insights. Self-awareness provides a meta-level perspective: you can reflect on why you feel a certain emotion, question the moral weight of a choice, or imagine futures where different actions lead to different outcomes. This capacity to reflect on reflection itself introduces a recursive depth. It's like having an internal watchtower from which you survey the mental landscape. From this watchtower, you can adjust your internal filters, improve your decision-making criteria, and refine the patterns through which you transform infinite mental possibilities into stable, meaningful realities.

In this sense, free will and moral agency are not mystical endowments separated from the natural order. Rather, they arise as subjective manifestations of the complexity-alignment principles that govern all stable outcomes. When you choose ethically, truthfully, and empathetically, you reduce internal cognitive friction and social complexity costs. This isn't mere moral goodness for its own sake—it's strategically sound complexity navigation at the individual level. Honesty with yourself—acknowledging personal flaws, biases, and fears—improves the accuracy of your mental filters. Honesty with others reduces social friction and enhances predictability and trust, making your environment more conducive to stable, beneficial patterns that reinforce your sense of agency.

The interplay between rational thought and emotional experience enriches this complexity-filtering mechanism. Rationality helps you evaluate options clearly, weighting long-term outcomes and systemic stability. Emotions, on the other hand, serve as complexity signals, guiding attention to areas of personal or ethical importance. Fear may highlight a potential threat or instability that needs resolution; empathy may draw attention to an opportunity for cooperation or kindness. By interpreting emotions not as irrational intrusions but as complexity cues, you integrate them into the filtering process. This synergy ensures that decision-making is not a cold calculation nor a blind emotional rush, but a balanced and adaptive approach that stabilizes your personal complexity landscape.

Creativity also enters the picture. When you conjure new ideas or solutions, you tap into a rich mental possibility space. Without a filtering mechanism, your mind could be overwhelmed by imaginative chaos. But through internal criteria shaped by ethics, aesthetics, feasibility, and personal values, you refine these sparks of imagination into coherent creations—artworks that convey beauty, proposals that solve problems, or personal goals that inspire growth. Creativity thrives when complexity is large enough to offer endless raw material but structured enough— through your mental filtering—for coherent outcomes to surface.

These principles have profound existential implications. Recognizing that your consciousness operates under the same structural logic that fosters stable galaxies or resilient ecosystems can reduce existential angst. If your mind and moral compass reflect universal patterns of complexity alignment, then you are not an outsider in a meaningless cosmos. Instead, you participate intimately in the universe's grand narrative of transforming infinite possibility into stable, meaningful manifestations. This recognition can imbue personal struggles with context and hope. Challenges become signals that existing filters need refinement, that you must integrate new information, adjust moral priorities, or deepen emotional understanding. Over time, each resolved challenge further aligns your inner complexity with sustainable patterns, fostering psychological resilience and moral maturity.

CHAPTER 6: CONSCIOUSNESS, AGENCY, AND SELF-AWARENESS (PART B)

Consciousness, as the subjective experience of complexity and its patterns, endows you with a powerful tool: foresight. By modeling various outcomes in your mind before acting, you can anticipate which options reduce friction and complexity costs. This anticipatory power is a defining feature of agency. Rather than reacting blindly to stimuli, you envision futures, weigh their coherence, and select paths that promise long-term stability and ethical congruence.

Free will, often debated as either an illusion or a mystical gift, finds a rational footing here. Will is "free" not in the sense of defying all laws, but in the sense of navigating a vast possibility space with meaningful criteria that reflect both rational assessment and moral concern. When confronted with moral quandaries—should you speak out against injustice, invest time in helping others, or remain indifferent—you consult internalized principles that mirror complexity's stable attractors. Ethical frameworks act as internal compasses, guiding you toward outcomes that, over time, prove more sustainable and fulfilling. Thus, free will becomes the lived experience of filtering complexity ethically and rationally at the personal scale.

This perspective also clarifies the role of self-discipline and moral growth. If your internal filtering mechanisms are initially crude—prone to selfish impulses or short-term thinking—your decisions may yield unstable, friction-laden outcomes. Recognizing these disappointments as feedback, you refine your moral compass and intellectual filters. The next time similar choices arise, you navigate complexity with greater skill, producing more stable, beneficial results. Over the years, this iterative improvement cultivates virtues like patience, honesty, and empathy. Such virtues, once understood as moral endowments, now reveal themselves as strategic refinements for handling complexity under ethical guidance.

Emotions, often doubted for their "irrationality," serve as valuable signals in this complexity management. Anxiety might indicate unresolved tension in your decision criteria, prompting you to seek additional information or reassurance. Compassion signals opportunities to reduce unnecessary friction between individuals, leading to stronger alliances and mutual support. Pride in a job well done suggests that the complexity filtering you applied worked effectively, reinforcing similar strategies in the future. By listening to emotions as complexity indicators rather than nuisances, you integrate their guidance into your decision-making framework, ensuring that choices resonate with both rational logic and heartfelt understanding.

The synergy between rational and emotional faculties also underlines why personal narratives—stories you tell yourself about who you are and what matters—shape how you approach complexity. A self-narrative that emphasizes ethical alignment and long-term coherence encourages you to interpret challenges as calls for better filtering rather than personal failures. This narrative choice reduces internal friction, making mental complexity more manageable and promoting psychological well-being. You find purpose in striving for coherence, knowing that each ethical decision aligns you with stable patterns that benefit you and those around you.

In relationships, this complexity-centered ethic transforms how you interact. Instead of exerting power through deception or manipulation—which might grant short-term gains but introduce long-term instability—you opt for transparent communication and genuine respect. By doing so, you predict more stable bonds, deeper trust, and richer collaborations. Friendships, partnerships, and familial ties flourish when complexity is not a battlefield of hidden motives but a playground of honest exploration, where everyone participates in reducing uncertainty. In such environments, love and loyalty become natural outcomes of ethical complexity management, not fragile hopes at the mercy of random forces.

In professional or creative endeavors, recognizing that complexity alignment fosters innovation and resilience can embolden you. Without fearing complexity, you approach intricate projects with confidence. Each setback signals a refinement opportunity. Colleagues who share these principles form teams that can handle unknown variables, quickly adapt to new information, and produce breakthroughs that stand the test of time. By embracing complexity instead of avoiding it, you contribute to a culture that thrives under uncertain conditions, ensuring stability and collective success.

This reasoning extends to your inner spiritual or existential quests. While the OK Model does not assert any religious claim, the realization that complexity alignment leads to stable, harmonious outcomes can resemble spiritual truths valued by many traditions. Some may find that living in accordance with ethical complexity principles mirrors aspects of compassion taught by spiritual paths. Others may find existential comfort in knowing that their moral struggles and triumphs are part of a logical pattern woven into the universe's structure. Such interpretations, while personal, illustrate the model's capacity to inform not just external actions but internal worlds of meaning and purpose.

Ultimately, by understanding your mind and moral sense as manifestations of complexity filtering, you see that self-awareness is more than a clever biological adaptation. It's a point of leverage, allowing you to consciously refine how you handle infinite possibilities. You are not a pawn tossed about by complexity; you are an agent who can surf its waves, extracting stable, beneficial patterns from the vastness of potential. Each choice you make, guided by honesty and foresight, confirms your role as a caretaker of complexity alignment, ensuring that your life's narrative arcs toward greater coherence, understanding, and well-being.

This realization can dissolve feelings of isolation or insignificance. Instead of fearing a meaningless cosmos, you understand that your personal growth, moral commitments, and creative endeavors resonate with fundamental structural imperatives. Awareness, free will, moral duty, and emotional richness interlock to form a stable complexity cycle at the personal scale. This cycle, continuously refining and improving through experience, parallels the grand narratives of galaxies finding stable orbits or societies cementing ethical norms.

In conclusion, embracing your consciousness and agency as complexity filters allows you to see your life as an ongoing, meaningful project. Strive to understand more, choose ethically, engage empathically, and remain open to continuous refinement. The rewards are not abstract promises but structurally sound outcomes: richer relationships, more dependable success in your endeavors, deeper self-understanding, and a resonant sense of belonging in a universe that itself favors stable, ethically guided complexity. This perspective affirms that the very essence of your consciousness—the interplay of thought, emotion, and moral judgment—is not an evolutionary fluke or a philosophical quandary. It's an essential feature of a universe in which everything coherent and beneficial can indeed emerge and sustain, including your own evolving story.

CHAPTER 7: INFINITE TESTABILITY, INFINITE REFINEMENT (PART A)

Understanding that complexity-driven systems can yield stable and coherent outcomes leads naturally to the idea that no explanation or model capturing this logic is ever final. If complexity is dynamic, evolving, and responsive to feedback, then any conceptual framework must also remain open to challenge, critique, and improvement. This principle—that the lens through which we interpret complexity can and should be tested infinitely—underscores the importance of infinite testability. It encourages a stance of perpetual refinement, an intellectual posture that sees new data, anomalies, and critical questions not as threats but as opportunities to deepen understanding.

Infinite testability suggests that the best intellectual tools are never static monuments of certainty. Instead, they are adaptive instruments, shaped and reshaped by experience, evidence, and debate. When confronted with unexpected phenomena or patterns that defy current logic, the proper response is not to defend the theory at all costs, but to integrate the new information, adjust assumptions, and produce a more nuanced explanation. This process mirrors how living systems adapt to changing environments: they do not cling to outdated strategies but evolve. In the realm of thought, infinite testability invites a similar evolutionary approach to knowledge.

The result is intellectual anti-fragility. A model or idea that can incorporate new findings and withstand scrutiny without crumbling becomes stronger, clearer, and more applicable. Each challenge refines the filters used to navigate complexity, reducing blind spots and eliminating hidden biases. Instead of fearing contradictions, infinite testability welcomes them as beneficial stressors, catalysts that highlight where refinement is needed. Over time, these cycles of test and adaptation produce conceptual frameworks that resonate more closely with reality's complexity.

Crucially, infinite testability aligns with the ethical imperative for openness and honesty. Embracing infinite testability means maintaining intellectual integrity: one must be prepared to admit when certain assumptions fail, when predictions miss the mark, or when a proposed mechanism proves too simplistic. This honesty fosters trust in the intellectual process itself. Just as societies prosper when trust and transparency reduce social friction, so too does knowledge prosper when ideas remain transparent, critiquable, and correctable. A closed, rigid theory might appear confident, but it risks disintegrating under the weight of a single counterexample. An infinitely testable model, by contrast, invites an indefinite sequence of probes that gradually reinforce its central insights or transform them into something better.

Consider how scientific revolutions have historically emerged from anomalies. When data stubbornly refused to fit established theories—be it the orbit of Mercury defying Newtonian predictions, or the blackbody radiation problem upending classical assumptions—new paradigms arose. These paradigm shifts weren't acts of intellectual defeat; they were triumphs of infinite testability. By not shielding theories from evidence, thinkers allowed fresh perspectives to arise, forging more comprehensive and robust understandings of reality. Infinite testability, then, is not just a principle of humility but a strategy for continuous intellectual progress.

In human affairs, from social policy to ethical frameworks, infinite testability similarly ensures that decisions and norms are not set in stone. As societies face emerging technologies, shifting cultural values, or environmental challenges, previous solutions may no longer suffice. Rather than stubbornly clinging to outdated doctrines, infinite testability encourages re-examining assumptions, gathering new data, and revising approaches. This adaptive strategy reduces long-term complexity friction, ensuring that moral codes and policies remain effective guides for evolving conditions.

This concept also resonates at the personal level. Individuals who understand infinite testability adopt flexible mindsets, welcoming feedback on their choices and beliefs. Criticism and unforeseen difficulties become signals prompting personal growth rather than threats to one's self-worth. Such a stance wards off dogmatism, defensiveness, and intellectual stagnation. The mind that embraces infinite testability is free to learn from mistakes, integrate insights from critics, and continually refine its moral compass and cognitive strategies.

CHAPTER 7: INFINITE TESTABILITY, INFINITE REFINEMENT (PART B)

Embracing infinite testability also fosters an intellectual culture where collaboration flourishes. When all ideas are open to examination and refinement, it becomes easier for researchers, policymakers, and thinkers from different fields to share their findings and integrate their expertise. Instead of defending territorial claims over pet theories, they collectively work to refine conceptual tools and produce more reliable predictions. This cooperative spirit resembles trust networks in societies: just as ethical coherence reduces social complexity friction, intellectual coherence and honesty reduce friction in the marketplace of ideas.

In practical terms, infinite testability encourages setting up ongoing experiments, simulations, and data-sharing platforms. Investigators design research not to confirm what they already believe, but to probe the boundaries of their assumptions. Negative results or unexpected outcomes become valuable clues. Rather than lamenting that a prediction failed, they celebrate having located a gap in understanding—an opportunity for refinement. Over cycles of this process, theoretical models become more attuned to reality, complexity filters become more accurate, and the outcomes they predict or guide become increasingly stable and beneficial.

Another benefit of infinite testability is that it inoculates against dogmatic stagnation. Many intellectual traditions have suffered when adherents refused to question core tenets. By contrast, a framework that mandates continuous testing and welcomes contradiction is inherently resilient. It cannot become a brittle orthodoxy because it thrives on the very challenges that would shatter a closed system. This intellectual anti-fragility ensures longevity and adaptability, mirroring how ecosystems survive by evolving with changing environments, and how societies endure by revising outdated practices.

At a moral and existential level, infinite testability provides comfort. Instead of fearing that cherished ideas might one day be disproven, individuals and communities can find solace in the knowledge that if old assumptions fail, better explanations will emerge. This perspective reduces anxiety about uncertainty. If everything can be tested infinitely and improved upon, then uncertainty isn't a void of despair but a frontier of discovery. Each resolution of anomaly deepens confidence, not in a static truth, but in the process of iterative refinement itself.

The logic of infinite testability also underscores that no single moment or solution is the final summit of understanding. Instead, progress unfurls as a continuous journey, where each stage of comprehension leads to new questions. This perpetual openness ensures that intellectual pursuit remains vibrant, creative, and hopeful. Knowledge does not settle into a quiet retirement; it remains an active participant in shaping the future, forging new alliances between disciplines, and informing ever more subtle and inclusive policies.

In a world where complexity is always present—be it in quantum fields, social dynamics, environmental stewardship, or personal moral growth—this adaptive, testable stance is both necessary and freeing. It allows humanity to face emerging challenges with confidence that no crisis must remain unsolvable. If current frameworks falter, infinite testability provides the route to improved models and strategies. If current moral or cognitive assumptions prove inadequate, continuous refinement ensures that more ethically coherent or cognitively robust principles will arise.

This stance resonates deeply with trust and openness. Just as trust in social contexts enhances stability, trust in the iterative, corrective power of open inquiry enhances the stability of our intellectual landscape. We trust that infinite testability keeps us from hardening into rigid dogmas. We trust that honest effort to confront anomalies leads us toward deeper, truer insight. And we trust that moral and cognitive improvements are always possible when guided by the willingness to test, critique, and adapt.

At its core, infinite testability is an ethic of humility and ambition combined. Humility, because it admits no final answers; ambition, because it aspires to refine and elevate understanding indefinitely. This balance mirrors ethical behavior at the social scale: a humility that respects complexity's unpredictability, and an ambition that strives for greater coherence. Together, they encourage a mindset eager to learn, ready to integrate new information, and determined to keep complexity a source of constructive patterns rather than a cause of paralyzing confusion.

In conclusion, infinite testability and infinite refinement ensure that our journey through complexity remains progressive. No victory is permanent, no failure is final. Each test and correction creates a richer tapestry of knowledge, a more reliable compass for navigating complexity. Embracing this logic transforms intellectual work into a living, evolving enterprise that grows stronger with each challenge, guided by a process that ensures adaptation, resilience, and the perpetual emergence of clearer, more ethically aligned perspectives.

CHAPTER 8: PRACTICAL APPLICATIONS AND PREDICTIVE POWER (PART A)

A conceptual framework that explains how complexity filters yield stable outcomes is more than a philosophical insight; it's a tool for navigating reality. The principles of complexity alignment, ethical coherence, and infinite refinement are not confined to abstract reasoning. They can be deployed as strategic assets in policy-making, organizational strategy, creative innovation, resource management, and personal decision-making. By transforming understanding into action, these ideas empower individuals and communities to shape their futures more confidently and ethically.

The predictive power inherent in complexity logic is one of its most valuable gifts. If patterns reflect stable complexity, then once you understand the conditions that foster stability, you can anticipate the outcomes of various interventions. This predictive capability relieves the anxiety of guesswork in complex scenarios. Instead of lurching from crisis to crisis, societies and organizations can plan proactively, testing scenarios, identifying harmonizing structures, and implementing measures that reduce friction and uncertainty. Over time, strategic applications of these principles build trust, improve efficiency, and open pathways toward long-term flourishing.

1. Policy-Making and Governance

In domains like governance and public policy, complexity alignment offers a systematic approach to handling infinite social possibilities. Policymakers frequently face an overwhelming array of data, interests, and proposed solutions. Without guiding principles, political processes may devolve into stalemates, corruption, or rash decisions that cause unintended harm. Complexity logic, however, suggests that policies formed through transparent debate, factual integrity, and moral consideration reduce complexity friction. By applying such ethical filters, policymakers can sift through countless proposals and reliably select those that stand the greatest chance of producing stable, beneficial outcomes.

Predictive power emerges when repeating this process over multiple policy cycles. If open consultations and truth-driven research consistently yield stable improvements—like more equitable resource distribution or resilient social safety nets—then future policies can be guided by this experience. Just as one trusts the method of proven engineering principles in constructing bridges, one can trust complexity-aligned policy-making when facing new, intricate dilemmas. This trust fuels a virtuous cycle: each success improves predictive confidence, prompting further investment in ethical complexity strategies.

2. Organizational Strategies and Corporate Decision-Making

At the organizational level, complexity alignment serves as a strategic compass. Businesses, NGOs, research institutes, and cultural groups all grapple with infinite tactical possibilities. Without a framework, decisions can drift aimlessly or be captured by short-term profit motives, internal politics, or secrecy. Complexity logic advises embedding ethical coherence—honesty in management, transparent accounting, fair treatment of employees and partners—into the organization's culture. Doing so reduces internal friction, enabling teams to work fluidly, adapt to market changes nimbly, and innovate more freely.

Predictive power in organizations manifests as better forecasting: stable complexity patterns repeat. If a company fosters trust, it can predict stable customer loyalty, reduced employee turnover, and smoother negotiations with suppliers. Over time, these positive feedback loops become tangible assets. Instead of relying on aggressive, opaque tactics that might yield one-off wins but create long-term instability, complexity-aligned strategies ensure lasting success and reputational strength. The organization learns to anticipate systemic responses, plan for resilience, and allocate resources optimally.

3. Resource Management and Crisis Prevention
Global and local resource management often suffers from short-term thinking, data misinterpretation, and power imbalances. Complexity alignment's core lesson—that stable, ethical coherence leads to predictable and beneficial outcomes—translates well into resource allocation and environmental stewardship. By applying transparent data-sharing, rigorous scientific methods, and inclusive stakeholder dialogues, communities can preempt scarcity crises or environmental collapses.

Predictive power in resource contexts emerges through iterative learning. If certain practices—like cooperative water-sharing agreements or transparent energy distribution policies—consistently yield stable resource availability, then stakeholders can trust these approaches when tackling future challenges. Instead of reacting with panic whenever droughts or energy shortfalls appear, decision-makers rely on the proven logic that honesty, empirical clarity, and fairness minimize complexity friction. Gradually, resource management becomes a domain where complexity is channeled into steady abundance rather than desperate competition.

—

CHAPTER 8: PRACTICAL APPLICATIONS AND PREDICTIVE POWER (PART B)

With complexity alignment and ethical coherence established as strategic assets, the path forward involves deploying these insights in increasingly intricate environments. The predictive power of complexity logic can guide actions even under conditions of uncertainty, offering ways to preempt pitfalls and enhance stability.

4. Cultural, Educational, and Social Innovations

When it comes to shaping cultural narratives, educational methods, or social projects, complexity alignment suggests that certain patterns of communication and engagement are more fruitful. Consider educational reforms that emphasize critical thinking, transparent evaluation, and inclusive dialogue. By reducing the complexity friction in learning—eliminating misinformation, promoting honest feedback between teachers and students—these reforms produce stable, self-improving academic communities. Predictably, they yield higher knowledge retention, better problem-solving skills, and more harmonious intellectual climates.

Cultural projects also benefit. Artistic communities that share resources openly, critique works constructively, and celebrate creative diversity find that stable complexity emerges organically, leading to robust cultural scenes that last generations. Predictive power appears in the ability to foresee that open workshops, fair intellectual property rules, and honest curation of artistic talents result in cultural ecosystems that adapt and evolve positively. Instead of suffering from hidden biases or exploitative patronage, complexity-filtered cultural networks repeatedly produce enduring masterpieces, thriving festivals, and evolving traditions.

5. Balancing Long-Term Strategies with Adaptive Flexibility
One challenge in complexity navigation is the tension between committing to long-term strategies and retaining the flexibility to adapt when unexpected changes arise. Complexity logic and predictive power help navigate this tension. By understanding which patterns foster stable outcomes, decision-makers can commit to ethical frameworks, open communication channels, and continuous data-sharing protocols that prepare them for surprises.

When a sudden crisis hits—a technological disruption, a resource shortage, or a cultural shift—those who have aligned with complexity logic and established predictive models can rapidly adjust. They do not start from scratch; they rely on proven filters and stable decision-making heuristics to reorient themselves. Predictive power doesn't guarantee exact foresight of every event, but it assures that complexity filters are well-calibrated to handle unforeseen variables. Thus, long-term visions and immediate responses become complementary rather than conflicting.

6. Integrating Multiple Perspectives and Expertises
Achieving stable outcomes in complex scenarios often requires integrating perspectives from multiple fields. Predictive power shines brightest when various domains—science, ethics,

technology, economics—contribute their filtering insights. If trust and ethical coherence guide these interdisciplinary collaborations, friction reduces, and patterns of stable problem-solving emerge.

For instance, a team tackling climate adaptation might bring together climatologists, farmers, engineers, policy analysts, and community leaders. Infinite potential solutions abound, but complexity alignment suggests focusing on transparent data, fair cost-sharing, and inclusive dialogue. The team can predict that by respecting each domain's knowledge, ensuring open debates, and adopting mutually beneficial goals, the final chosen measures will yield stable environmental resilience. Over time, repeated successes confirm that interdisciplinary trust and ethical standards produce consistently superior outcomes, reinforcing the predictive power of complexity logic.

7. Addressing Skepticism and Motivating Participation

Though complexity logic and predictive power promise strategic advantages, some may remain skeptical. They might question whether moral alignment and open communication genuinely yield better predictions. The best response to such doubt is to conduct pilot studies and small-scale experiments. Show that in a controlled environment—like a local community project—applying complexity alignment (honest data, fair decision rules) leads to the anticipated stable results.

As these demonstrations accumulate, skepticism erodes. People become willing participants in complexity-friendly initiatives, contributing their talents and ideas more openly. Over time, a collective memory forms: attempts guided by complexity logic and predictive modeling consistently perform better than manipulative, secretive, or unethical approaches. This cumulative evidence steadily shifts cultural norms, making complexity alignment a recognized hallmark of effective and sustainable action.

8. Opportunities for Technological and Scientific Advancements

Predictive power extends beyond social and economic spheres into research and innovation. Scientists who adopt complexity alignment frameworks can design experiments that more accurately forecast phenomena. Engineers can model infrastructure projects—bridges, grids, networks—anticipating stress points and preventing catastrophic failures before they happen. By factoring in transparent data-sharing, honest risk assessments, and inclusive stakeholder consultations, large-scale projects can be planned with greater certainty of stable outcomes.

In emerging technologies—artificial intelligence, biotechnology, quantum computing—complexity logic and predictive modeling become invaluable. These fields contain vast unknowns. However, applying ethical filters and trust-based research cultures reduces misinformation, accelerates consensus on safety standards, and improves the reliability of innovation processes. Over iterative cycles, complexity-friendly tech policies predict safer deployments, fair benefits distribution, and resilient innovation ecosystems.

9. Cultivating Individual Mindsets for Predictive Approaches

At the personal scale, understanding predictive power in complexity management helps individuals tackle their own challenges more systematically. When facing career decisions, health regimes, or financial planning, infinite possibilities can overwhelm. Complexity logic guides you to use honesty (about your strengths and limitations), openness (to learn from diverse inputs), and ethical considerations (avoiding exploitative shortcuts) to refine your options into stable, fulfilling life choices.

Over time, personal experience with complexity alignment leads to growing confidence. As you observe that truthfulness and empathy reliably produce better personal outcomes—less relational conflict, more stable career trajectories, deeper satisfaction—you trust the model's logic even more. This trust emboldens you to attempt more ambitious goals, knowing that complexity need not be an adversary but a resource from which stable patterns emerge predictably under correct guidance.

10. Continuous Improvement of Predictive Frameworks

Predictive power is not static. As new data and scenarios arise, filters and heuristics evolve. This ongoing improvement ensures that complexity management techniques remain relevant in changing environments. Markets may transform, cultural values shift, technologies mature. The logic of complexity alignment dictates that these transitions be met not with rigid doctrines, but with adaptable predictive frameworks that integrate each new lesson.

This cycle of refinement ensures that predictive methodologies themselves never stagnate. Instead, they evolve toward greater accuracy, inclusivity, and ethical sensitivity. By continually testing predictions, absorbing negative results, and recalibrating strategies, predictive power grows stronger and more reliable, reinforcing trust in the complexity alignment process.

11. Achieving Greater Stability and Confidence Through Prediction

Predictive power is ultimately about confidence—not blind faith, but reasoned assurance that by following complexity alignment principles, outcomes turn out more stable and beneficial. Whether you're drafting a public policy, launching a scientific expedition, organizing a cultural exchange, or planning a personal project, the logic behind complexity-driven predictions provides calmness, clarity, and courage. The assurance that ethical coherence and honest filtering transform complexity from a puzzling maze into a navigable landscape is comforting and empowering.

At every scale, from personal decisions to global initiatives, the ability to predict stable patterns reduces anxiety. Instead of fearing the unknown, complexity alignment shows that unknowns can be mapped, tested, and guided toward harmonious results. Over time, this mastery of complexity through predictive models can reshape how individuals, organizations, and societies approach even the most daunting challenges, fostering trust and encouraging steady progress.

In conclusion, the practical applications and predictive power derived from understanding complexity alignment translate intellectual insights into actionable strategies. They validate the approach's relevance, showing that the same logic that grounds ethical coherence and stable cosmic structures can also guide daily action, social reforms, and innovative breakthroughs. Embracing this predictive capability transforms complexity from a source of apprehension into a strategic advantage, helping all actors—individuals, communities, institutions—steer toward stable and uplifting futures.

CHAPTER 9: CHALLENGES, CRITIQUES, AND FUTURE DIRECTIONS (PART A)

A framework that aspires to universality and broad applicability cannot avoid scrutiny. Whenever a conceptual model claims to illuminate how complexity produces stable outcomes, ethical alignments, and predictive power, skeptics rightfully ask challenging questions. Their critiques sharpen the model, highlighting areas needing formalization or clearer empirical connections. Far from an impediment, these questions and objections serve as valuable feedback loops, guiding ongoing refinement and ensuring the framework does not devolve into dogma.

One common concern revolves around the model's universality. Observers may wonder if it's too elastic, capable of explaining any result retroactively, thus risking tautology. To address this, the model's proponents must devise criteria for empirical testing. They must identify specific predictions or constraints that, if not met, would require revising fundamental assumptions. Critics may demand that the model not only absorb new data easily but also specify conditions under which its logic can fail.

Without such conditions, detractors might argue that the model's strength is an illusion of interpretive flexibility rather than actual explanatory power.

Another area of skepticism involves the absence of a unified mathematical formalism. Words like "complexity," "ethical coherence," and "stable patterns" are evocative but could remain fuzzy if not translated into quantitative measures. Critics might urge the development of complexity indices, trust metrics, or formal game-theoretic models that capture how ethical considerations reduce friction and select stable outcomes. Such formalization would allow controlled simulations and experiments—either computational or in social laboratory settings—offering clear predictions and testable scenarios. By demanding mathematical and empirical rigor, critics push the model toward concrete ground where failures and successes become unmistakable.

A further challenge may arise from cultural and historical contexts. Some might say that ethical principles and stable complexity outcomes vary too widely across eras and societies for any universal pattern to hold. They might argue that certain historical examples of societies thriving under seemingly manipulative or opaque systems undermine the claim that ethical coherence is always superior. In response, refining the model would involve investigating exceptions, identifying what temporary conditions allowed unethical complexity management, and determining whether such conditions are inherently unstable long-term. These historical anomalies act like stress tests on the model, forcing it to detail when and why certain behaviors that appear to contradict complexity alignment might momentarily prosper but eventually falter.

Philosophers could raise another critique: the model naturalizes ethics, portraying moral principles as structural necessities rather than autonomous moral laws. They may fear that this reduces the moral domain to a utilitarian calculus of complexity minimization. To address such philosophic concerns, the model's advocates must engage deeply with moral theory. They might show that while ethical coherence emerges as a strategic advantage in complexity navigation, this does not preclude richer moral philosophies, human dignity arguments, or notions of intrinsic moral worth. Instead, complexity alignment could be presented as providing a rational substrate upon which deeper moral convictions can stand, not as a simplistic replacement for moral reasoning itself.

Some scientists and theorists may object that the model has yet to produce a breakthrough prediction that differs significantly from established theories in any given domain. Without unique predictive content—cases where the model forecasts a phenomenon that other frameworks cannot—the model might seem like a restatement of well-known principles cloaked in new terminology. This critique encourages the formulation of bold, differentiating hypotheses. For instance, propose scenarios in social governance or resource management where applying complexity alignment principles leads to outcomes no conventional theory would anticipate. If these predictions are validated, skeptics would have concrete reasons to take the model's novel logic seriously.

Another angle of critique emerges from the realm of complexity research itself. Complexity science is a rich field with its own metrics, computational models, and empirical findings. Some complexity experts may ask how exactly the model's logic improves upon existing complexity theories—like those involving network dynamics, emergence in adaptive systems, or evolutionary game theory. They might challenge the model to integrate seamlessly with known complexity tools, adding ethical coherence and trust as quantifiable variables rather than abstract notions. By doing so, they push the model to interface with established methodologies, paving the way for rigorous comparative studies, simulations, and cross-disciplinary collaborations.

A related challenge involves working through actual case studies. It's one thing to describe theoretically how ethical coherence reduces friction and leads to stable complexity patterns; it's another to show this in practice. Critics may demand in-depth analyses of specific historical transitions—such as the gradual establishment of transparent governance in certain countries—and measure whether complexity alignment principles truly predicted stable improvement. Another case might be to examine organizations that shifted from secretive, exploitative practices to open, ethical ones, tracking how complexity indicators (like employee turnover, litigation rates, innovation metrics) improved predictably after reforms. The careful compilation of such evidence would address skeptics who require demonstrable cause-and-effect relationships.

In addition, critics might raise the issue of unfalsifiability if every outcome can be rationalized post hoc. To counter this, the model's proponents must show that certain outcomes are either improbable or structurally discouraged under complexity alignment. For example, they could argue that persistent large-scale corruption in a supposedly complexity-aligned system is fundamentally incompatible and should collapse or force a system reconfiguration. If evidence shows stable corruption persisting indefinitely without collapse, this would contradict the model's logic. Thus, by highlighting scenarios that would disprove or seriously challenge the model, the framework gains scientific credibility, since it can be proven wrong if reality fails to match its structural predictions.

CHAPTER 9: CHALLENGES, CRITIQUES, AND FUTURE DIRECTIONS (PART B)

Beyond addressing immediate criticisms, there is the matter of future directions. If the model's advocates embrace infinite testability, they must also chart a research agenda that transforms its abstract insights into concrete, measurable approaches. Such an agenda would entail:

1. Formalization Efforts:
Efforts to produce mathematical formulations could focus on representing infinite potentials (S) as high-dimensional state spaces, complexity filters (Φ) as operators or functions that prioritize certain configurations, and stable outcomes (P) as attractors or equilibrium solutions. By translating these notions into equations, inequalities, or topological structures, researchers can run simulations, test predictions under controlled conditions, and compare results against actual data. This formalization would allow complexity alignment principles to be studied quantitatively, making it possible to report statistical correlations between trust-based policies and long-term resource stability, or between ethical norms and the longevity of cooperative

institutions.

2. Interdisciplinary Experiments and Case Studies:
Another fruitful direction lies in designing interdisciplinary experiments that explicitly apply complexity logic to real-world scenarios. Consider forming research consortia where economists, sociologists, ethicists, and complexity theorists collaborate. They could select specific societal problems—like devising transparent budget allocations in a municipal project—and then measure the complexity reduction and stability gain from ethical interventions. By systematically documenting these interventions, researchers can identify patterns that confirm or challenge the model's claims. Over multiple experiments, if complexity alignment reliably enhances stability and predictability, skepticism diminishes.

3. Longitudinal Analyses of Societal Transitions:
A more ambitious project could involve historical and longitudinal studies, examining how ethical reforms correlate with increased stability across decades or centuries. Archival research might reveal that when certain transparent governance measures were adopted, the complexity of managing trade or diplomatic relations eased over time, resulting in fewer conflicts and more robust economic growth. Conversely, if certain unethical structures persisted without collapse, investigators would be forced to refine the model, discovering exceptions or additional variables that need incorporation. Such historical depth ensures the model remains grounded in empirical reality rather than theoretical elegance alone.

4. Global Collaborations and Complexity Observatories:
Given that complexity alignment principles aim at universal applicability, establishing complexity observatories—institutions dedicated to monitoring complexity metrics in different sectors—could be beneficial. These observatories might track data on

trust indicators, transparency indices, ethical compliance rates, and system outputs (such as market volatility or social conflict frequency). By comparing regions or institutions that implement complexity-friendly policies against those that do not, patterns emerge. If the predicted stability gains consistently appear in complexity-aligned systems, these observatories would provide an evidence base to guide future reforms and validate the model's predictive claims.

5. Philosophical and Ethical Dialogues:
Engaging with moral philosophers, theologians, and cultural critics remains essential. While the model suggests that ethical coherence is structurally favored, it does not automatically resolve all moral questions. Philosophers can probe whether certain moral values, while complexity-friendly, still need justification beyond mere structural advantage. They may ask if complexity alignment ensures genuine moral progress or merely stable outcomes that resemble moral ideals. By discussing these subtleties, the model's ethical dimension can deepen, accommodating richer moral philosophies and refining its interpretation of what constitutes "good" in complexity terms.

6. Incorporation of Technological Advances in Complexity Research:
The rapid growth of computational capabilities and data analytics tools offers vast opportunities. Machine learning algorithms could simulate various complexity scenarios, testing which ethical parameters improve system stability. AI agents could be trained under different moral constraints, examining whether honesty and empathy-like policies outperform deceptive or short-sighted strategies. If consistent results show that ethical constraints lead to more successful adaptation in AI simulations, it provides yet another evidence stream supporting the model's logic. This technological approach also aids in fine-tuning complexity metrics and identifying subtle thresholds or tipping

points where ethical coherence makes the decisive difference between stability and collapse.

7. Continuous Feedback from Anomalies and Surprises:
Maintaining intellectual honesty means that when anomalies appear—cases that defy predictive patterns—researchers do not sweep them under the rug. Instead, they highlight anomalies, treating them as priority investigations. Each anomaly might signal a missing variable or an overlooked social factor. For instance, what if a society achieves temporary stability through restricted information flow and controlled propaganda, defying the expectation that honesty and transparency are essential? Studying such exceptions might reveal transitional phases or special conditions where complexity alignment works differently, prompting revisions to the model or its assumptions. By cherishing anomalies, the approach ensures perpetual evolution and refinement, proving that infinite testability is not just a slogan but a lived principle.

8. Encouraging Public Engagement and Intellectual Openness:
The framework's potency also depends on how widely it is communicated and understood by the public. If the notion that ethical coherence fosters stable complexity patterns becomes common knowledge, citizens may demand greater transparency in governance, honesty in organizational leadership, and empathy in cultural exchanges. As ordinary people participate in complexity alignment—voting for transparent policies, supporting honest media, embracing ethical consumer choices—they generate more data points for researchers and improve the system's overall predictive fidelity. The synergy between public understanding, scholarly refinement, and practical application forms a feedback loop that continuously elevates the framework's credibility and influence.

In essence, the future directions revolve around a collaborative, iterative, and open-ended approach. By acknowledging critiques, forging new research paths, integrating moral depth, leveraging technology, embracing anomalies, and involving the public, the model evolves from a theoretical lens into a robust, testable paradigm. Over time, if these efforts bear fruit, skepticism recedes, replaced by cautious confidence and inspired curiosity. Each refinement cycle adds resolution to the complexity map, each debate clarifies a subtlety, and each successful prediction deepens trust in the model's logic.

As critics help sharpen the arguments and anomalies guide improvements, the model demonstrates resilience and adaptability. Instead of fearing the future, it anticipates it, ready to adapt and grow. This dynamic attitude ensures that complexity alignment and ethical coherence remain compelling and useful guides, not relics of a static worldview. Embracing challenges and welcoming critiques thus fuels intellectual evolution, ensuring that the framework's logic remains not only intact but progressively more illuminating as humanity's understanding advances.

CHAPTER 10: A POST-SCARCITY MINDSET AND GLOBAL FLOURISHING (PART A)

The vision of a world in which material scarcity recedes and humanity collectively thrives is no longer confined to utopian speculation. Growing knowledge, technological innovations, and the deepening understanding of complexity alignment suggest that a future of global flourishing is not merely possible but structurally supported. By reducing the friction and uncertainty that stifle creativity, cooperation, and equitable resource distribution, societies can transition from zero-sum struggles to a post-scarcity mindset—one in which resources, knowledge, and cultural achievements become more accessible and abundant than previously imagined.

To understand the path toward this abundance, consider how complexity alignment principles guide every decision affecting resource flows, social frameworks, and cultural exchanges. The complexity of managing planetary resources—energy grids, water supplies, agricultural lands—might seem daunting, but ethical coherence and transparency turn complexity into a navigable asset. Instead of hoarding information or manipulating markets for short-term gain, openness and fairness channel complexity into stable patterns. Over time, such stable patterns lead to more efficient production methods, more resilient supply chains, and more sustainable consumption practices.

A post-scarcity mindset begins with acknowledging that many scarcities are products of mismanagement, mistrust, or hidden agendas rather than actual material shortages. When societies commit to transparent data-sharing about resource availability, environmental conditions, and technological capabilities, they reduce the informational asymmetries that cause panic and competition. This transparency—like trust in social or economic domains—acts as a complexity filter. It sifts through infinite resource allocation scenarios and favors those that produce stable equilibrium states: widespread access to essential goods, minimal waste, and improved well-being. Over iterative refinements, these equilibrium states gain permanence, embedding a new cultural norm: that no one need suffer deprivation if complexity is ethically navigated.

Such a norm radically alters cultural psychology. Historically, fear of scarcity fueled conflicts, colonial expansions, environmental devastations, and class struggles. Once societies demonstrate that trust-based global collaborations can provide clean energy at scale, distribute nutritious food with negligible losses, and secure potable water for all, people begin to let go of zero-sum thinking. With their core needs met predictably, individuals feel freer to pursue educational, artistic, and entrepreneurial ventures that further enrich the collective. Freed from the grind of desperation, human creativity flourishes, leading to exponential cultural and intellectual growth. The infinite possibilities of human ingenuity are no longer hindered by constant anxiety over basic sustenance.

This evolution also reframes the meaning of "wealth." Under scarcity conditions, wealth often measures how much one can accumulate at others' expense. Under post-scarcity conditions, wealth becomes a function of how many beneficial outcomes one can catalyze, how creatively one can engage with complexity, and how broadly one can share knowledge and cultural accomplishments. Ethical coherence ensures that increases in one domain (like a breakthrough in energy storage) don't result in exploitation but in widely distributed advantages. Resource abundance ceases to be a private fortress; it becomes a common platform from which everyone can reach greater intellectual and moral heights.

Embracing a post-scarcity mindset doesn't imply naivety about environmental limits or the complexity of global coordination. Rather, it encourages addressing these challenges head-on with tools that complexity alignment provides. For instance, if advanced manufacturing techniques can produce goods with minimal waste and distributed fabrication reduces transportation costs, then societies can design production networks that adapt dynamically to changing demands. Ethical complexity filters ensure these networks remain balanced, preventing resource bottlenecks or price manipulations that reintroduce friction.

On a global scale, consider the distribution of knowledge itself. If trust and openness guide the exchange of research findings, educational materials, and cultural works, then a post-scarcity mindset in information emerges. People across geographic and economic divides can access cutting-edge knowledge without gatekeepers artificially constraining it. This informational abundance stimulates problem-solving capacity in every region, allowing local communities to tailor global insights to their specific contexts. Over time, less developed regions experience leaps in development without traditional exploitation patterns, as the complexity filters—ethical research collaborations, fair licensing agreements, and translation initiatives—predictably produce stable intellectual and cultural enrichments.

Such intellectual abundance supports ethical and cultural pluralism. Freed from struggling over basic resources, communities can cultivate their unique identities, traditions, and artistic expressions, contributing to a tapestry of human experience that thrives on diversity rather than succumbing to homogenization born of scarcity competition. Predictive power, harnessed through complexity logic, suggests that as trust and empathy scale globally, cultural exchanges yield stable patterns of mutual respect and cross-pollination. Each cultural tradition refines and enriches its complexity filters in dialogue with others, amplifying creativity and mutual understanding.

CHAPTER 10: A POST-SCARCITY MINDSET AND GLOBAL FLOURISHING (PART B)

The post-scarcity mindset also reshapes the role of institutions. Governments and international organizations, guided by transparency and complexity alignment, shift from crisis management to proactive stewardship. Instead of reacting to famines, energy shortages, or sudden market crashes, they anticipate where friction might arise and apply ethical, data-driven interventions in advance. Over iterative cycles, these anticipatory measures confirm their predictive value, building public trust and reinforcing the model's core premise: stable complexity emerges and endures under conditions of honesty, empathy, and knowledge-sharing.

This stability, in turn, reduces the emotional toll of living under constant uncertainty. When people believe that global cooperation can ensure sufficient food, energy, and healthcare, anxiety recedes. Without the fear of starvation or catastrophic conflict, space opens for deeper intellectual pursuits, spiritual growth, and cultural innovation. The human spirit, freed from the weight of relentless competition for limited resources, can invest more energy into exploring the moral, aesthetic, and philosophical dimensions of existence. A post-scarcity world encourages humans to ask not how to survive the next shortage, but how to improve moral reasoning, broaden artistic expression, and deepen scientific inquiry.

Economic models change accordingly. Where once countless resources were spent guarding property, enforcing exclusionary patents, or gaming financial systems, in a post-scarcity context those habits lose purpose. Complexity alignment predicts that systems cluttered by mistrust and cunning exploitation are inherently unstable. As societies reap the dividends of opensource technologies, fair licensing, and collaborative supply chains, exploitative tactics find less fertile ground. Investors, producers, and consumers learn that long-term stability and wealth arise from ensuring broad access and fairness. This shift in economic rationality is profound: success no longer stems from monopolizing resources, but from enhancing everyone's capacity to navigate complexity effectively.

Moreover, environmental sustainability becomes more achievable. When fundamental ethics dictate that future generations deserve as much stability as present ones, environmental protection and restoration become natural complexity filters, preventing ecologically destructive practices that generate long-term friction. Renewable energy networks, regenerative agriculture, and circular manufacturing align so well with stable complexity principles that their adoption becomes predictable. Over time, these environmentally conscious strategies outcompete wasteful, polluting methods, resulting in ecosystems that recover vitality, biodiversity, and resilience. The planet itself benefits as human stewardship aligns with complexity logic, ensuring predictably stable ecological outcomes.

At the cultural level, as scarcity-driven paranoia recedes, communities embrace moral narratives that celebrate cooperation, compassion, and curiosity. Instead of mythologies of scarcity and conflict, stories of collective triumph over complexity emerge—tales of how knowledge-sharing solved droughts, how transparent governance prevented corruption, how inclusive debates bridged seemingly unresolvable cultural rifts. These narratives reinforce trust and encourage the next generation to believe in the power of complexity alignment as a guiding ethic. With each repeated success story, skepticism wanes, and the culture internalizes post-scarcity principles as common sense rather than radical experiments.

Individual lives also transform under post-scarcity conditions. Freed from the struggle over basic necessities, people can take more strategic personal risks—starting ventures that prioritize social good, pursuing educational paths aligned with moral passions, or devoting time to community art projects. The complexity logic assures them that when honesty and mutual respect guide their interactions, stable relationships and supportive networks form. Predictably, emotional well-being improves, as does the sense of life's worth. Children grow up less stressed about shortages and conflicts, absorbing a worldview that complexity is manageable and often a source of shared opportunity, rather than a threat that must be conquered.

While achieving such a state may seem distant, the key realization is that every step towards ethical coherence, every policy that encourages honest data-sharing, every intercultural dialogue that reduces misunderstanding, lays another brick in the path toward post-scarcity. Each local success story—be it a city that solved housing issues transparently or a network of farmers that pooled resources fairly—increases collective predictive power and trust in complexity alignment. Over time, these incremental gains accumulate, transforming global mindsets and reducing friction at larger scales. Eventually, this cumulative process can flip the narrative from scarcity-driven fears to confidence in sustainable abundance.

In essence, the post-scarcity mindset and the ensuing global flourishing do not materialize out of thin air. They are earned through consistent application of complexity alignment principles. By insisting on honesty as a baseline, ensuring open flows of information, fostering empathy in negotiations, and continually refining predictions and strategies, humanity can gradually unlock the stable abundance that complexity logically supports. Once scarcity no longer dictates economic models or cultural anxieties, the human spirit can focus on what truly matters—moral improvement, scientific exploration, artistic creativity, and the deep appreciation of shared existence.

This long-term vision is neither naive nor unattainable. It is grounded in the rational observation that complexity alignment repeatedly proves itself in smaller scales and simpler domains. When scaled up and applied consistently, it can foster a stable global environment where fear and insecurity give way to trust and growth. The journey may be incremental, marked by trials and setbacks, but each setback is just another complexity test, guiding further refinements. The direction, once recognized, seems inevitable: toward a future where human potential is freed from the chains of scarcity, and where the complexity of our world, channeled ethically, becomes a source of enduring prosperity and cultural enlightenment.

CHAPTER 11: PERSONAL AND PHILOSOPHICAL REFLECTIONS (PART A)

At the heart of complexity alignment lies the individual's experience. While grand visions of ethical coherence guiding societies or post-scarcity abundance reshaping global relations are inspiring, these outcomes ultimately derive from the choices, emotions, and moral reasoning of countless individuals. Each person navigates complexity at an intimate scale: within their minds, relationships, and personal moral struggles. Understanding how the logic of complexity applies to one's internal world—shaping purpose, integrity, and emotional well-being—transforms abstract principles into lived realities.

When you recognize that stable complexity arises from honesty, empathy, and rational filtering of possibilities, you gain a fresh lens through which to interpret personal challenges. Instead of viewing moral dilemmas as arbitrary burdens, you see them as opportunities to enhance coherence. Every decision—whether to help a friend, invest time in self-improvement, or respond ethically to a difficult situation—can be understood as complexity navigation. Choosing compassion, for instance, reduces friction in interpersonal dynamics, cultivating trust and predictability that extend beyond the immediate interaction. Over time, these repeated ethical choices accumulate, forming stable patterns of personal conduct that feel authentic and deeply satisfying.

This alignment reassures that ethical behavior isn't an artificial constraint on freedom; it enriches freedom by making your range of meaningful choices more robust and rewarding. When lying or exploiting others might seem advantageous in the short term, complexity logic suggests such tactics introduce internal and external friction that destabilizes outcomes. By contrast, truthfulness and fairness serve as personal complexity filters, consistently yielding stable friendships, reliable partnerships, and a sense of inner peace. Instead of fretting about moral actions out of fear of societal judgment or divine punishment, you embrace them as rational steps toward stable, beneficial personal complexity states. Honesty and kindness become strategic allies in crafting a life characterized by emotional security and meaningful connections.

This perspective also addresses existential questions that often plague reflective minds. When confronted with the vastness of the universe or the uncertainty of life's purpose, the logic of complexity alignment offers a grounding point. You exist within a reality that favors stable outcomes. Your capacity for reason, moral intuition, and empathy are not random flukes but features of a complexity-rich environment that nurtures coherence. This insight can alleviate existential angst. If complexity alignment repeatedly proves effective at all scales, then your moral instincts and intellectual endeavors sit firmly within a grand narrative of order emerging from possibility. You belong to a universe where striving for ethical coherence isn't just personally fulfilling, but cosmically resonant.

Emotions, often considered tumultuous or irrational, find new interpretation as signals guiding complexity navigation. Fear may warn you of impending instability, pushing you to seek additional information or resources. Compassion pulls you toward opportunities to reduce friction in social ties. Gratitude signals the successful alignment of complexity in your life—when you feel grateful, it's often because you've recognized a stable, beneficial pattern: supportive friends, a fulfilling job, a peaceful home. By treating emotions as complexity indicators rather than mysterious intrusions, you integrate them more constructively into decision-making. Emotional literacy and rational analysis become partners, ensuring that neither cold logic nor impulsive feeling dominate, but rather a harmonious interplay that reflects stable complexity in your mental processes.

Through this lens, personal growth becomes a continuous refinement process. Mistakes and regrets no longer symbolize personal failings etched into your character; they are indicators that previous filters were imperfect. A bad decision that caused unnecessary pain can be understood as a filter malfunction—perhaps you lacked sufficient empathy, rushed judgment, or fell prey to misinformation. Learning from these experiences refines your internal criteria, ensuring that next time you face similar complexity, you have better chances of choosing outcomes that foster stability. Moral maturation arises naturally from iterative complexity handling, each lesson making your internal filters more ethically aligned.

CHAPTER 11: PERSONAL AND PHILOSOPHICAL REFLECTIONS (PART B)

Recognizing that complexity alignment offers existential reassurance also allows you to move beyond defensive postures. Instead of spending mental energy rationalizing poor choices or resisting constructive criticism, you accept feedback as fuel for improvement. When you stop fearing that acknowledging errors undermines your worth, acknowledging them becomes liberating. Errors highlight where complexity filters failed to yield stable outcomes. With each correction, your moral compass and intellectual judgment become more accurate, guiding you more reliably in future scenarios. Over time, this iterative refining of personal filters transforms uncertainty into a pathway of continuous moral and intellectual evolution.

This approach also fosters humility. If complexity alignment is an ever-refining process, then no individual can claim perfect moral vision or flawless judgment. Everyone is engaged in ongoing calibration. Such humility reduces the combative urge to impose one's views aggressively. Instead, you approach moral disagreements and intellectual debates with curiosity and openness, eager to discover what complexities others have navigated and what lessons their perspectives might hold.

This humility enhances dialogue and collaboration. Instead of entrenching defensively when challenged, you treat challenges as opportunities to refine your understanding. Friendships, family bonds, professional networks—all these social fabrics strengthen when mutual humility and constructive critique guide their complexity management.

On a spiritual or existential level, this stance might resonate with traditions that value compassion, patience, and inner wisdom. While the model itself makes no religious claims, many spiritual paths emphasize virtues that align strikingly well with complexity logic: kindness reduces conflict, honesty fosters trust, empathy bridges cultural divides. By seeing these virtues not as external commandments but as structural best practices, you find renewed appreciation for spiritual teachings that highlight them. In essence, your moral growth aligns with ancient wisdom that also recognized the pragmatic and deeply human advantages of ethical living.

Another key dimension is how this logic reframes your relationship with ambition and success. If stable complexity outcomes arise from honest filtering processes, then "success" ceases to mean winning by any means necessary. Instead, success involves generating patterns that last, patterns that do not crumble under the weight of deception or exploitation. Personal ambitions—whether they involve career milestones, creative achievements, or community contributions—become long-term projects guided by transparency and care. Predictably, such ambitions yield more sustainable satisfaction. The excitement of short-term triumphs at others' expense pales compared to the lasting fulfillment of contributing to stable, ethically aligned complexity states that benefit many.

In intimate relationships, complexity alignment encourages openly sharing hopes, fears, and vulnerabilities. By reducing emotional opacity, partners navigate shared complexity more effectively. Each honest conversation, each empathic act, ensures that friction diminishes and trust grows. Over time, this trust allows even deeper emotional bonds, as both individuals find security in the predictability and kindness that ethical coherence provides. If conflicts arise, they are not catastrophic but solvable puzzles—moments for re-tuning the complexity filters that govern communication. Such relationships mature resiliently, weathering challenges with grace and mutual understanding.

For creative endeavors, acknowledging complexity alignment encourages you to embrace experimentation without terror of failure. Every attempt—whether writing a poem, designing software, or devising new educational methods—is a complexity test. Some attempts will yield immediate stable outcomes, while others will reveal overlooked complexities requiring adjustments. With each refinement, the creative process becomes more intuitive and less fraught with anxiety. You trust that ethical clarity and intellectual honesty will guide you toward results that stand the test of time, enhancing artistic longevity and cultural impact.

This personal and philosophical vantage also clarifies how to approach mortality and legacy. While everyone's lifespan is finite, your actions contribute to stable complexity patterns that outlive you. Honest mentorship, ethical leadership, creative solutions, and kind gestures form part of a tapestry that continues to stabilize complexity in others' lives. Your influence, shaped by complexity alignment, extends beyond your individual existence. This notion can lessen the existential sting of impermanence, as you see your moral and intellectual contributions as threads woven into the evolving complexity fabric that future generations inherit.

In confronting global challenges—climate threats, cultural tensions, resource distribution—you may feel small as an individual. But remembering that complexity alignment works at every scale, you see your role not as insignificant but as part of a global complexity cycle. Your ethical, honest acts, however localized, still contribute to the broader pattern of reducing friction and enabling stable solutions. Encouraged by this realization, you engage with public debates, support equitable policies, and advocate for reasoned, compassionate responses. Even if you cannot solve massive crises alone, your consistent alignment with ethical complexity principles helps normalize these patterns, inspiring others and tipping the scales toward collective progress.

In summary, by internalizing complexity alignment principles and understanding their role in shaping stable outcomes, you transform your inner landscape. Your decisions carry more weight and clarity, your emotional life becomes more coherent, and your moral growth aligns with structural necessities that benefit both yourself and others. Rather than treating morality as a set of rigid commandments or existential order as a distant hope, you see both as integrally connected to the logic of complexity. This recognition instills confidence, calmness, and purpose. You become a participant in a grand interplay, assured that honest efforts and empathic reasoning resonate with fundamental forces that guide reality toward stable, enriching states.

Thus, personal and philosophical reflections lead to a more confident stride through life. Aware that complexity alignment is not just idealistic talk but a rational imperative that consistently proves beneficial, you navigate moral choices, intellectual challenges, emotional struggles, and existential questions with newfound poise. Each step forward, each lesson learned, every ethically grounded decision made, enhances the coherence of your individual narrative and strengthens the larger web of relationships and cultural patterns to which you belong.

CHAPTER 12: EVERYTHING'S OK —EMBODYING THE LENS (PART A)

Recognizing that complexity alignment and ethical coherence bring about stable outcomes at every scale—physics, societies, personal life—instills both understanding and responsibility. Awareness alone cannot bring change; it must be translated into lived practice. To embody the lens means integrating these insights into daily habits, moral choices, professional endeavors, and intellectual pursuits. Instead of treating complexity alignment as a distant framework, you make it a personal ethic, a guiding principle that informs how you think, communicate, solve problems, and interact with others.

Embodying this lens begins with a shift in perspective. When facing complexity—be it a complicated negotiation at work, a conflict in personal relationships, or a creative challenge—you pause and recall that complexity is not a foe but a resource. Instead of panicking at uncertainty or defaulting to zero-sum strategies, you ask: which actions reduce friction, foster trust, and promote stable, beneficial outcomes for all involved? This question transforms your approach from crisis management to constructive navigation. Over time, it becomes second nature, a quiet voice reminding you that honesty and empathy reduce complexity costs and yield patterns that last.

This embodiment also involves cultivating intellectual humility. The model suggests continuous refinement: no idea or solution is above scrutiny. Adopting this practice personally means welcoming constructive criticism rather than dreading it. When colleagues challenge your project plan, when loved ones question your assumptions, or when new data contradicts your predictions, you respond not with defensiveness but with curiosity. Openness to new information and willingness to adjust your filters maintains resilience in your personal strategies. Each revision in response to critique isn't a defeat but a step toward greater coherence and predictability in your outcomes, reinforcing your faith in the logic of complexity alignment.

On a moral and emotional level, embodying the lens involves recognizing emotions as signals that guide complexity handling. When you feel anxiety about a decision, ask what friction or unknown factors feed that anxiety. Could seeking more data, discussing openly with trusted parties, or rethinking the ethical dimensions alleviate it? When sadness arises from witnessing harm or injustice, interpret it as an alarm indicating complexity mismanagement—perhaps certain ethical principles are being ignored, causing unnecessary conflict. Acting to restore trust or reintroduce transparency can help resolve that sadness, making your emotional state a meaningful feedback loop rather than a source of despair. With time, you learn to read your emotions not as random disturbances but as informative guides in complexity negotiation.

Embodying the lens also means rethinking personal ambition. Instead of chasing short-term rewards at all costs, you consider the long-term stability and ethical resonance of your goals. Ask whether your ambitions—professional success, financial gain, recognition—contribute to stable complexity patterns or if they rely on exploitative shortcuts. Aligning your ambitions with stable complexity might involve choosing career paths that emphasize fairness, innovation that benefits many, or community engagement that shares knowledge. While such choices may sometimes appear slower or less flashy, they predictably produce more enduring fulfillment, reduced stress, and a stronger sense of integrity.

In interpersonal relationships, embodying the lens translates into more authentic communication. When disagreements surface, rather than trying to "win" at the expense of understanding, you focus on transparency and empathy. By explaining your viewpoints honestly, admitting uncertainties, and listening openly, you reduce unnecessary friction. Conflict shifts from a destabilizing force to an opportunity to refine shared complexity filters. Over repeated interactions, trust deepens, dialogues become more productive, and stable relational patterns emerge —friendships that weather crises, partnerships that endure hardships, family ties that strengthen over generations.

CHAPTER 12: EVERYTHING'S OK —EMBODYING THE LENS (PART B)

Embodying this perspective also encourages proactive anticipation rather than reactive problem-solving. Instead of waiting for crises to force changes, you maintain a watchful awareness of emerging complexities, ready to adjust your approaches early. This mindset applies broadly—if you're leading a project at work, you don't wait for severe conflicts to erupt before implementing transparent decision-making protocols; you start with them. If you're shaping community initiatives, you incorporate open forums and ethical guidelines from the outset, so that trust and stability build naturally rather than needing costly repairs later. Over time, you learn to see potential friction points before they become disruptive, guiding systems gracefully toward stable outcomes.

This forward-looking attitude reduces anxiety in uncertain times. Rather than dreading the unknown, you view it as a playing field where complexity alignment principles will help you find coherence. When technological disruptions appear, you approach them with confidence, knowing honest exploration and ethical considerations will steer you toward workable solutions. When social or cultural shifts cause tension, you trust that transparent dialogue and inclusive reasoning can restore equilibrium. This reduces fear and cultivates a sense of calm strength, an understanding that while absolute certainty is impossible, stable patterns can emerge predictably when guided by the right filters.

On a deeper moral level, embodying the lens involves acknowledging that you have a role in maintaining not just your personal well-being, but the ethical fabric of your environment. Each time you choose honesty in a situation where deceit might have given quick advantage, you reinforce a stable complexity pattern that can influence others. Each time you invest effort in empathetic listening during a heated debate, you model complexity-friendly behavior that others may adopt. The cumulative effect of countless individuals behaving ethically and openly can shift the entire tone and trajectory of organizations, communities, and larger networks. By taking personal responsibility in this way, you contribute to a collective evolution that moves from fragile arrangements to robust, trust-based systems.

This recognition of personal responsibility does not imply burdensome perfectionism. Instead, it encourages humility: no one will flawlessly embody these principles at every turn. Mistakes occur; conflicts arise; temptations to exploit or conceal information will surface. Embodying the lens means accepting these imperfections as natural tests. Each misstep highlights a gap in your understanding or an overlooked factor in your complexity handling. Instead of becoming disheartened, you use these experiences to refine your mental filters, adjust your strategies, and try again. Over time, this iterative self-improvement leads to greater ease and competence, just as repeated experiments lead scientists closer to reliable theories.

At the personal scale, this approach can transform everyday experiences. Tasks that once felt dauntingly complex—learning new skills, navigating career transitions, resolving family tensions—now appear as instances of complexity that can be tamed through honesty, empathy, and rational filtering. You learn to predict that a fair and transparent negotiation yields better outcomes than secretive maneuvering, that patience and listening solve more conflicts than aggressive confrontation. As successes accumulate and confirm these predictions, your confidence grows. Complexity ceases to intimidate; it invites you to participate fully and consciously in shaping reality.

Beyond practical utility, embodying the lens fosters a sense of meaningful purpose. If complexity alignment repeatedly proves that ethical coherence underpins stable patterns, then striving for moral integrity is more than a personal virtue—it's a cosmic resonance. Your moral growth and intellectual refinement are not isolated personal achievements but part of a larger tapestry where stable complexity emerges through countless acts of honesty, empathy, and reason. Recognizing that your choices harmonize with fundamental principles of order and sustainability can provide profound existential comfort. You no longer search for meaning as a desperate quest in a random universe; you find it in the purposeful navigation of complexity toward enduring good.

This existential comfort does not dispense with life's challenges. Hardships remain, losses occur, and difficult moral crossroads appear. But even in adversity, you know that complexity alignment logic suggests pathways to regain stability. Honesty about a personal failure can restore trust after a setback. Empathy in response to suffering can rebuild fractured relationships. Rational recalibration after unexpected outcomes can improve your strategies. Each challenge, painful though it may be, becomes a lesson that enhances future coherence.

Over time, as these principles become ingrained habits, you embody the lens not as a forced discipline but as a natural style of thought and action. Ethical reasoning becomes your default mode, transparency your reflex, empathy your steady companion. Stressful situations become less destabilizing, since you trust the underlying logic that has guided you successfully before.

This trust in the process radiates outward, influencing others who witness your calm integrity, your willingness to adapt, and your compassionate approach to complexity. They may ask about your methods, learn from your example, or contribute their own insights, creating positive feedback loops that strengthen complexity alignment at larger scales.

In essence, embodying the lens means merging understanding with being. It's no longer about studying complexity logic or moral coherence as interesting concepts; it's about living them daily. Just as musicians internalize music theory until playing becomes intuitive, you internalize complexity alignment until ethical complexity navigation becomes second nature. The theoretical lens dissolves into direct perception: you see complexity for what it is, sense the stable paths through it, and choose accordingly, not out of obligation but because it feels right, rational, and deeply connected to the structures underlying all stable phenomena.

This transformation grants a quiet assurance: everything, at its core, can be guided to coherence. Whether grappling with personal grief, collective reform, scientific puzzles, or artistic quests, you trust that complexity is not your enemy. With honesty, empathy, rational foresight, and openness to continual refinement, you can steer complexity toward outcomes that are supportive, enlightening, and uplifting. This assurance is not naive optimism; it's a confidence earned by observing complexity alignment principles succeed in countless trials, from small personal interactions to large-scale initiatives.

In conclusion, embodying the lens means that the logic of complexity alignment and ethical coherence is no longer external knowledge but internalized wisdom. It shapes your responses to life's intricacies, makes your moral stance consistent, and imbues your efforts with dignity and hope. From this vantage point, the phrase "everything's ok" transcends a reassuring cliché. It becomes a statement of profound truth: when complexity is navigated with honesty, empathy, and rational adaptation, stable and meaningful patterns emerge predictably, allowing both individuals and communities to flourish in harmony with the world's inherent logic.

Epilogue

In the pursuit of understanding and purpose, we have journeyed through insights that connect the human mind's awareness, moral principles, and the structures of reality itself. Complexity, once feared as overwhelming confusion, emerges as a dynamic tapestry where coherent patterns can be reliably discovered and nurtured. By embracing trust, empathy, rational inquiry, and ethical coherence as essential filters in managing complexity, we find that what might have seemed intractable problems can yield stable, beneficial outcomes.

This recognition is neither sentimental nor naïve. It is grounded in repeated confirmations: honesty reduces friction, fairness enhances predictability, empathy encourages constructive alliances, and transparent communication eases the passage of infinite possibilities into tangible achievements. Each test of these principles—be it in personal struggles, societal reforms, scientific endeavors, or intercultural exchanges—provides further evidence that complexity alignment is not a temporary convenience but a structural truth. Over time, as more endeavors confirm this pattern, confidence grows. Complexity alignment becomes a trusted guide, a quiet assurance whispering that stable solutions are attainable.

The transformations induced by this worldview are subtle yet profound. Individuals facing ethical crossroads no longer feel adrift in moral ambiguity. Instead, they appreciate that virtuous acts serve as strategic moves in complexity's grand game, consistently delivering more satisfying, enduring outcomes.

Communities, awakened to the advantages of open dialogue, shared knowledge, and fair governance, unlock reservoirs of creativity and resilience that stagnant distrust had long suppressed. Scientific inquiries advance with less dogmatic friction, as researchers willingly refine theories and absorb anomalies, confident that infinite testability and adaptation produce deeper and more accurate insights.

On an existential level, knowing that human consciousness, moral intuition, and cultural wisdom resonate with fundamental complexity alignment relieves the pressure to find meaning in arbitrary constructs. Meaning emerges naturally from coherent patterns that consistently arise when honesty and compassion guide complexity's potential. This frees one from the shadow of existential despair or the tyranny of nihilism. While not every question has a ready answer, the process of seeking solutions through alignment ensures that confusion need not breed hopelessness. Challenges become portals to improved coherence, not traps of defeat.

None of this claims perfection or finality. Imperfections remain, misunderstandings persist, and crises will occur. Yet, armed with an understanding that complexity responds favorably to certain ethical and intellectual filters, humans can approach adversity without cynicism or helplessness. Every setback, every disappointment, every surprise offers clues for better complexity navigation in the future. This ethic of infinite refinement, learned from observing complexity alignment in nature and society, assures that no failure is ultimate, no flaw irreversible.

In this spirit of ongoing exploration, the insights gained form a living philosophy rather than a static doctrine. By repeatedly verifying that ethical coherence leads to stable outcomes, people come to trust these principles not because tradition or authority demands it, but because experience endorses it. Over generations, this trust recalibrates cultural narratives, emphasizing mutual understanding, long-term thinking, and inclusivity. As global challenges arise, societies prepared with honesty, openness, and adaptive reasoning can face them with steady hands.

Standing at this vantage point, one can appreciate that while complexity offers no shortcuts and no guaranteed utopias, it also withholds nothing essential to achieving stability and meaning. The logic that let electrons settle into orbital shells and galaxies weave majestic patterns is the same logic that allows individuals and communities to form lasting, enriching patterns of cooperation and moral guidance. By embracing honesty, reason, and empathy as complexity filters, we align ourselves with a fundamental principle of reality, and thereby secure a foothold in a universe that, at its core, favors coherence over chaos.

In the calm of such recognition, one finds not only intellectual reassurance but a gentle moral compass. The knowledge that ethically guided complexity filters produce stable, positive outcomes encourages us to carry these principles forward into future endeavors. As the world evolves, as new technologies and crises emerge, as relationships deepen and cultures converge, this understanding arms us with both a method and a motive. Complexity alignment becomes second nature—an abiding faith in the convergence of rationality and compassion, ensuring that whatever lies ahead can be approached with confidence, dignity, and an enduring sense of hope.

B.T.C.
12-12-24

Aimee,
Your kindness shines. ✳
Thank you,
Brooke

Printed in Great Britain
by Amazon